VIEWPOINT

STUDENT'S BOOK 1A

MICHAEL MCCARTHY
JEANNE MCCARTEN
HELEN SANDIFORD

CAMBRIDGE
UNIVERSITY PRESS

CAMBRIDGE
UNIVERSITY PRESS

University Printing House, Cambridge CB2 8BS, United Kingdom

One Liberty Plaza, 20th Floor, New York, NY 10006, USA

477 Williamstown Road, Port Melbourne, VIC 3207, Australia

314–321, 3rd Floor, Plot 3, Splendor Forum, Jasola District Centre, New Delhi – 110025, India

79 Anson Road, #06–04/06, Singapore 079906

Cambridge University Press is part of the University of Cambridge.

It furthers the University's mission by disseminating knowledge in the pursuit of education, learning and research at the highest international levels of excellence.

www.cambridge.org
Information on this title: www.cambridge.org/9781107601512

First published 2012
Reprinted 2019

Printed in Great Britain by CPI Group (UK) Ltd, Croydon CR0 4YY

A catalogue record for this publication is available from the British Library

ISBN 978-0-521-13186-5 Student's Book 1
ISBN 978-1-107-60151-2 Student's Book 1A
ISBN 978-1-107-60152-9 Student's Book 1B
ISBN 978-1-107-60277-9 Workbook 1
ISBN 978-1-107-60278-6 Workbook 1A
ISBN 978-1-107-60279-3 Workbook 1B
ISBN 978-1-107-60153-6 Teacher's Edition 1
ISBN 978-1-107-63988-1 Classroom Audio 1
ISBN 978-1-107-62978-3 Classware 1

Cover and interior design: Page 2, LLC
Layout/design services and photo research: Cenveo Publisher Services/Nesbitt Graphics, Inc.
Audio production: New York Audio Productions

Authors' acknowledgements

The authors would like to thank the entire team of professionals who have contributed their expertise to creating *Viewpoint 1*. We appreciate you all, including those we have not met. Here we would like to thank the people with whom we have had the most personal, day-to-day contact through the project. In particular, Bryan Fletcher for his incredible vision, publishing ability, and drive – we deeply appreciate his confidence in us and our work; Sarah Cole, for her extraordinary editorial flair, market knowledge, technical skills, and superb direction of the project; Mary Vaughn for her usual outstandingly perceptive comments on our drafts and her excellent contributions to the material; Desmond O'Sullivan for his skills in managing the project successfully with unfailing good humor; Karen Davy for her tireless attention to detail; Catherine Black for her invaluable and timely help in the proofing stages; Graham Skerritt and Sabina Sahni for their detailed editorial comments; Dawn Elwell for her flawless design and production skills and especially her never-ending patience; Ellen Shaw for sharing her expertise so generously and for her continued support, which we value; Lorraine Poulter for her assiduous and supportive role in the creation of the Workbook; Sue Aldcorn for her work on creating the Teacher's Edition; Peter Satchell for his careful editorial support; Lisa Hutchins for making the audio program happen; Rachel Sinden for her role in setting up the online component. Carol-June Cassidy for her meticulous work with the wordlists; Tyler Heacock and Kathleen Corley, and their friends and family for the recordings they made, which fed into the materials; Ann Fiddes and Claire Dembry for their corpus support; Andrew Caines for corpus research support; Mike Boyle for contributing the articles in Units 4 and 7; Melissa Good for arranging access to the English Profile wordlists; Jenna Leonard, Sarah Quayle, and Helen Morris for making all kinds of things happen; Dr. Leo Cheng and Mercy Ships for the interview and photographs in Unit 5; Chris Waddell for the interview and photographs in Unit 12.

We would also like to express our appreciation to Hanri Pieterse and Janet Aitchison for their continued support.

Finally, we would like to thank each other for getting through another project together! In addition, Helen Sandiford would like to thank her husband, Bryan, and her daughters, Teia and Eryn, for their unwavering support.

In addition, a great number of people contributed to the research and development of *Viewpoint*. The authors and publishers would like to extend their particular thanks to the following for their valuable insights and suggestions.

Reviewers and consultants:
Elisa Borges and Samara Camilo Tomé Costa from **Instituto Brasil-Estados Unidos**, Rio de Janeiro, Brazil; Deborah Iddon from **Harmon Hall** Cuajimalpa, México; and Chris Sol Cruz from **Suncross Media LLC**. Special thanks to Sedat Cilingir, Didem Mutçalıoğlu, and Burcu Tezvan from **İstanbul Bilgi Üniversitesi**, İstanbul, Turkey for their invaluable input in reviewing both the Student's Book and Workbook.

The authors and publishers would also like to thank additional members of the editorial team: John Hicks, Lori Solbakken, and our **design** and **production** teams at Nesbitt Graphics, Inc., Page 2, LLC and New York Audio Productions.

Thank you to the models as well as all those who allowed us to use their homes and businesses for our Lesson C photographs, especially Nina Hefez; Tokyo Eat, the restaurant at the Palais de Tokyo, Paris, France; Panam Café, Paris, France; Thanksgiving grocery store, Paris, France; and Majestic Bastille Cinéma, Paris, France. Special thanks to the photographer, Fabrice Malzieu, for his skill, direction and good humor.

And these Cambridge University Press ***staff*** *and* ***advisors:***
Mary Lousie Baez, Jeff Chen, Seil Choi, Vincent Di Blasi, Julian Eynon, Maiza Fatureto, Keiko Hirano, Chris Hughes, Peter Holly, Tomomi Katsuki, Jeff Krum, Christine Lee, John Letcher, Vicky Lin, Hugo Loyola, Joao Madureira, Alejandro Martinez, Mary McKeon, Daniela A. Meyer, Devrim Ozdemir, Jinhee Park, Gabriela Perez, Panthipa Rojanasuworapong, Luiz Rose, Howard Siegelman, Satoko Shimoyama, Ian Sutherland, Alicione Soares Tavares, Frank Vargas, Julie Watson, Irene Yang, Jess Zhou, Frank Zhu.

Viewpoint Level 1 *Scope and sequence*

	Functions / Topics	Grammar	Vocabulary	Conversation strategies	Speaking naturally
Unit 1 **Social networks** pages 10–19	• Ask questions to get to know someone • Talk about friends and social networking habits	• Use the present tense, *tend*, and *will* to talk about habits	• Personality traits (e.g. *open-minded, pushy, talkative*) • Formal verbs (*obtain, withhold, accuse*)	• Ask questions to find out or check information • Use *And, But,* and *So* to start questions which link back to what the previous speaker said	• Questions with answers *page 138*
Unit 2 **The media** pages 20–29	• Talk about the influence of the media and celebrities • Share views on the impact of TV, online videos, and video games	• Use defining and non-defining relative clauses to give and add information • Use *that* clauses to link ideas	• Nouns and prepositions (*increase in, impact on*) • Formal expressions (*complex issue*)	• Use *which* clauses to comment on your own and others' statements • Use *You know what . . . ?* to introduce a comment on what you're going to say	• *which* clauses *page 138*
Unit 3 **Stories** pages 30–39	• Talk about life lessons and experiences • Tell stories about your childhood	• Use the past tense and present perfect forms • Use the simple past, past perfect, and past perfect continuous	• Expressions for school-related experiences (*count toward a grade*) • Verbs (*slip, tug,* etc.)	• Interrupt a story you are telling to make a comment and then come back to it • Use *(It's) no wonder* to say something is not surprising	• Auxiliary verbs *page 139*
Checkpoint 1 Units 1–3 pages 40–41					

Listening	Reading	Writing	Vocabulary notebook	Grammar extra
Reasons for ending friendships • Four people talk about solutions to relationship problems *But is it fair?* • Two students debate whether it is fair for employers to check out job applicants online	*Future college students and employees, beware!* • An article about the importance of posting only appropriate content online	• Write a script for a debate over whether or not employers should judge applicants by their online profile • Plan an argument • Contrast ideas and arguments • Avoid errors with *whereas*	*The right choice!* • Identify new vocabulary as formal or informal	• Questions • Frequency expressions • State verbs *pages 144–145*
It's really interesting that . . . • Five people discuss the effects of TV on young people *They're just games* • A professor delivers a lecture on violence and the media	*Not just a game* • An article about the impact of violent video games on young people	• Write a paragraph in an essay about whether songs with violent lyrics should be banned • Use topic sentences • List ideas • Avoid errors with listing expressions	*What an effect!* • When you learn a new noun, find out what prepositions are used with it	• Verbs in subject and object relative clauses • Using *that* clauses • *what* clauses *pages 146–147*
It just goes to show . . . • Three conversations about life lessons *How friendly are people?* • Three students describe the people in their cities	*Saturday* • A short story about a woman who suddenly feels invisible	• Write a narrative article about a positive or negative experience with people • Brainstorm and plan • Use verbs to structure an article • Avoid errors with the past perfect	*Catch up!* • Write a definition to help you remember a new expression	• Time expressions with the simple past and present perfect • Time expressions with the past perfect *pages 148–149*

Checkpoint 1 Units 1–3 pages 40–41

	Functions / Topics	Grammar	Vocabulary	Conversation strategies	Speaking naturally
Unit 4 **Working lives** pages 42–51	• Discuss and give advice on finding and changing jobs • Share opinions about perks and benefits offered by employers • Discuss and prepare to answer interview questions	• Use countable and uncountable nouns • Generalize and specify using definite and indefinite articles	• Verb + noun collocations on the topic of finding a job (*achieve a goal*) • Word families (*solve – solution*)	• Show your attitude toward what you say with *-ly* adverbs • Use *As a matter of fact* or *In fact* to give new information that you want to emphasize, or to correct what someone assumes or expects	• Word stress *page 139*
Unit 5 **Challenges** pages 52–61	• Talk about world issues and ways to help • Share wishes, hopes, and regrets about the world • Hypothesize on making the world a better place	• Use conditional sentences to talk about hypothetical events in the present or past • Use *wish* and *hope* to talk about wishes, hopes, and regrets	• World problems and solutions (*eradicate poverty*) • Word building (*devastate, devastation, devastated*)	• Suggest possible scenarios or ideas with *What if . . . ?, suppose,* and *imagine* • Use *I suppose* to show that you're not 100 percent sure	• Shifting word stress *page 140*
Unit 6 **Into the future** pages 62–71	• Talk about the future of money, technology, clothing, travel, entertainment, and everyday life • Give a presentation	• Describe future events with *be going to, will, may, might,* and the present • Use modal verbs for expectations, guesses, offers, necessity, requests, etc.	• Expressions used in giving presentations (*As you'll see on the slide.*) • Nouns for people (*climatologists*)	• Use *would* or *'d* to soften your opinions • Respond with expressions such as *I think so, I don't think so,* and *I guess not*	• Silent consonants *page 140*

Checkpoint 2 Units 4–6 pages 72–73

Listening	Reading	Writing	Vocabulary notebook	Grammar extra
The best perks • Five people discuss and give examples of perks and benefits offered to employees *Interview rules* • Five applicants are interviewed for a job	*Career help: What questions should I ask at a job interview?* • An article outlining questions a job applicant should and shouldn't ask during an interview	• Write a personal statement for an application form • Use nouns in formal writing • Avoid errors with uncountable nouns	*Meet that deadline!* • When you learn a new word, write down its collocations	• Making uncountable nouns countable • More about uncountable nouns • More about the definite article *pages 150–151*
What would you give away? • Three people talk about ways to help others *Inspiring people* • An interview with a doctor about his work with the charitable organization Mercy Ships	*On the Mercy Ships* • An interview with Dr. Leo Cheng, whose volunteer work with Mercy Ships changes lives in developing countries	• Write an email inquiry about volunteering • Use *it* as subject and object • Avoid errors with verb forms	*Wealthy = rich* • When you learn a new word, write down its synonyms or a paraphrase of it	• Continuous forms for conditions • *even if* and *unless* to talk about conditions • Use of *wish* with *would* • Strong wishes with *If only* *pages 152–153*
Going cashless – the pros and cons! • Two friends discuss the advantages and disadvantages of a cashless society *Future entertainment* • Four conversations about entertainment in the future	*What does the future look like?* • Four short news articles about developments and changes that could occur in the future	• Write a one-paragraph article about how our everyday life will be different in the future • Use modal verbs with adverbs • Structure a paragraph with topic, supporting, and concluding sentences • Avoid errors with adverbs	*Present yourself!* • Create an "idea string" for a new expression by thinking of different ways you can use it	• Plans and intentions with *be going to* and *will* • Present forms in clauses that refer to the future • More on necessity modals • Possibility modals in the affirmative and negative *pages 154–155*
Checkpoint 2 Units 4–6 pages 72–73				

Unit 1

Social networks

In Unit 1, you . . .

- talk about friends and social networking.
- use the present tense, *tend,* and *will* to talk about habits.
- ask questions to find out or check information.
- use *And, But,* and *So* in follow-up questions.

Lesson A *Speed-friending*

1 Getting to know each other

A CD 1.02 **Read the article. Why do people go to speed-friending events? What happens at this kind of event?**

Make New Friends and Network Fast!

These days we live life in the fast lane. We insist on fast food, quick service, high-speed downloads, instant messaging, and immediate responses. So why should we spend time making new friends? At a speed-friending event, you have just a few minutes to ask and answer questions before moving on to the next person. If you find people you'd like to get to know better, you can contact them after the event. Here are the kinds of questions that people ask.

1. How do you like to spend your free time?
2. What music are you listening to these days?
3. What was your most valuable possession as a child? And now?
4. Can you say no to chocolate?
5. When did you last stay out after midnight? Where were you?
6. Who's your favorite celebrity?
7. Have you ever won a prize or a contest?
8. What word describes you best?

About you

B Pair work **Take turns asking and answering the questions in the article.**

C **Write six interesting questions you'd like to ask at a speed-friending event. (For help with questions, see page 144.)**

How often do you go out with your friends?

D Class activity **Hold a speed-friending event in class. You have two minutes to ask each person your questions.**

2 Vocabulary in context

A 🔊 CD 1.03 **Listen. Tanya is describing people she met at a speed-friending event. Who do you think she will get in touch with again? Who won't she contact? Say why.**

Word sort

B Complete the chart with personality traits from Tanya's descriptions. Add more ideas.

I like people who are . . .	I don't like people who are . . .	I don't mind people who are . . .
open-minded		

Vocabulary notebook
See page 19.

About you

C Pair work **Do you know anyone with the personality traits in your chart? Take turns asking and answering questions.**

A Do you know anyone who is open-minded?
B Actually, my sister is very open-minded. She always listens to new ideas.

3 Viewpoint What makes a good friend?

Group work **Discuss the questions. Do you share the same views on friendship?**

- Think of three good friends. How would you describe them?
- Are there things about your friends or people you know that you don't like?
- How do friendships differ? Is it possible to be equally close to everyone?
- Would all your friends get along if they met one another?
- What do you think about speed-friending as a way to make new friends?

"Well, . . . my friend Martha is really sweet. She . . . "

In conversation . . .

You can use *Well, . . .* to take time to think.

Lesson B *Networking*

1 Grammar in context

A Class survey **Read the information. What percentage of your class uses these methods of communication every day? Vote on the methods you use, and complete the chart.**

How do you keep in touch?
Most people use several different ways to keep in touch. Here are the percentages of young people who use these methods of communication every day.

The percentage of young people who . . .		Your class
talk on a cell phone	70%	
send text messages	60%	
use instant messaging	54%	
use social networks	47%	
talk on a landline	46%	
send email	22%	

B CD 1.04 **Listen. Four people talk about how they communicate. What methods of communication do they use?**

We asked four people how they like to communicate. Here's what they said.

Jeff Gordon, 25

"I go on my social networking site five or six times a day. I'll log in when I'm taking a break. I like to check out my friends' pages and see what they're up to."

Victoria Garza, 40

"Personally I use email, but my kids are constantly texting. Occasionally my son will email someone like my sister, but with friends he tends to text."

David Smith, 31

"At work I'm on the phone all the time, but when I'm traveling, I normally use my laptop to make calls over the Internet. It doesn't cost anything, so . . ."

Sarah Wang, 19

"Every once in a while, I'll instant message with a friend. Some of my friends don't use IM, so mostly I just call on my cell to catch up with them."

About you

C Pair work **Find things in the interviews that you do and don't do. Tell a partner.**

"I go on my social networking site a lot, like Jeff. And I . . ."

2 Grammar Talking about habits

Figure it out

A Find sentences in the interviews with a similar meaning to the ones below. Rewrite the sentences, changing the words in bold. Then read the grammar chart.

1. With friends he **usually texts.**
2. Every once in a while, I **instant message.**
3. My kids **text all the time.**
4. When I **travel,** I normally use my laptop.

The present tense, *tend*, and *will*

Grammar extra
See page 145.

To talk about habits, you can use the simple present, the verb *tend*, or the modal verb *will*. Here, *will* does not have future meaning.

Mostly I ***call*** *on my cell. I****'m*** *on the phone all the time. My friends* ***don't use*** *IM.*

My son ***tends to*** *text. He* ***doesn't use*** *IM. Occasionally he****'ll email*** *someone.*

You can use the present continuous for a "longer" activity that happens at the same time as another habit.

When ***I'm traveling****, I normally use my laptop to make calls.*

You can use *always* and *constantly* with the present continuous for a habit that is noticeable or more frequent than is usual.

My kids ***are constantly texting****.*

In conversation . . .

People often use *will / 'll* in statements to talk about their habits. Questions and the negative forms *will not / won't* are rarely used in this meaning.

B Complete the conversations with a correct form of the verbs given. Then practice.

1. *A* How do you normally catch up with your friends? By phone?
   B Yeah. I _________ (tend / call) them when I'm taking my lunch break.
   A Yeah? I _________ (not call) my friends much. We _________ always _________ (email) each other, so . . .

2. *A* How much time do you spend on your social networking site?
   B I _________ probably _________ (will / spend) a few hours a day on it. I _________ (tend / use) it to make plans with friends. Mostly I _________ (check out) my friends' photos and stuff.
   A Yeah? I'm not on one. But occasionally I _________ (will / get) invites from people. But I _________ (not reply) to them.

3. *A* What do you mostly use your cell phone for? Texting?
   B Yeah. I _________ constantly _________ (text) my kids to find out where they are.
   A That's funny. In my family, we _________ (not text) a lot. We _________ (tend / talk). Like, my sister regularly _________ (call) me after dinner when she _________ (watch) TV.

About you

C Pair work **Write your own answers to the questions in Exercise B. Then take turns asking the questions and giving your own answers.**

D Group work **Prepare a short presentation about your family's communication habits to give to your group. Listen to your classmates' presentations, and ask questions.**

"Mostly I text my friends and family. My dad'll text me when he's working, and . . ."

3 Speaking naturally Questions with answers See page 138.

Lesson C *And why's that?*

1 Conversation strategy Finding out or checking information

A How would you feel if someone "unfriended" you (removed you from their list of friends on a social networking site)? Would you take it personally and be offended?

B CD 1.07 **Listen. What does Stan think about "unfriending" someone? How do you think Alexa feels about it?**

Stan I ran into Tammy today. She's really upset.
Alexa Oh, yeah? And why's that?
Stan Because I "unfriended" her.
Alexa Oh, that's awkward. How did she find out?
Stan I'm not sure, actually.
Alexa Huh. So why did you "unfriend" her?
Stan Well, it was nothing personal. It's just that every once in a while, you know, when I'm updating my profile, I'll remove people – if we haven't been in touch for some time.
Alexa But you emailed her, right? I mean, you let her know?
Stan No. I didn't think she'd be offended.
Alexa So you just delete people that you're not in touch with?
Stan Yeah. It's no big deal.

C Notice how Alexa asks some questions to find out new information.

She asks other questions in the form of statements to check information or her understanding of what was said or done. Find examples of both types of questions in the conversation.

"And why's that?"
"But you emailed her, right?"

D CD 1.08 **Complete the rest of Stan and Alexa's conversation with the questions in the box. Then listen and check. Practice with a partner.**

Alexa So has anyone ever "unfriended" you?
Stan You mean, taken me off their friends list? I don't think so.
Alexa ______________ It wouldn't bother you?
Stan No. I wouldn't mind at all. ______________
Alexa It's not *bad*. It's just Tammy didn't do anything wrong.
Stan ______________
Alexa Well, if they post obnoxious comments, for example.
Stan Hmm. ______________
Alexa Well, yeah. That's probably a good reason, too.
Stan Right. ______________
Alexa I don't know. Just make sure you never "unfriend" me! OK?

a. So you think it's bad, then?
b. And it's OK when you stop dating?
✓ c. So has anyone ever "unfriended" you?
d. But you'd be fine with it if they did?
e. So when *is* it OK, do you think?
f. But what should I do about Tammy?

2 Strategy plus Linking with *And, But,* and *So*

CD 1.09 You can start questions with ***And, But,*** or ***So*** to link back to things the previous speaker said. It makes the conversation "flow."

A CD 1.10 **Underline the best question to continue each conversation. Then listen and check your answers. Practice with a partner.**

1. *A* Have you ever removed someone from your list of friends online?
   B Actually, I don't have one. I'm not on a social networking site.
   A **And you just tend to add people? / So how do you keep in touch with people?**
2. *A* Do you think it's OK to "unfriend" people?
   B Oh, yeah. People do it all the time, I'm sure.
   A **Yeah. But why do they do it? / So they never remove anyone?**
3. *A* What would you do if someone deleted you from their friends list?
   B It depends. I probably wouldn't say anything.
   A **But you'd say something if it was a good friend? / And you'd call them, right?**

About you

B Pair work **Ask and answer the questions. Can you continue each conversation?**

3 Listening and strategies Reasons for ending friendships

A CD 1.11 **Listen to the first part of four conversations. What would each person say the problem is with his or her friendship? Number the issues 1–4. There are two extras.**

_____ We've lost touch.
_____ My friend is too serious.
_____ My friend posts annoying stuff on my wall.
_____ My friend is two-faced.
_____ We can't agree on things.
_____ We don't like each other's friends.

B CD 1.12 **Listen again. Circle the best question to continue each conversation.**

1. a. So you don't agree on *anything*?
   b. But do you agree on politics?
2. a. But she never posts photos, right?
   b. And does she post obnoxious comments, too?
3. a. But why does she do that?
   b. So does she talk about you behind your back?
4. a. So you mostly call each other?
   b. So she just dropped you?

C CD 1.13 **Listen to the complete conversations. Check your answers. What solutions do the speakers have for their friendship problems?**

About you

D Pair work **Agree on six good reasons for ending a friendship and the best ways to do it.**

A *Well, if you don't agree on anything, it's probably a good reason to end a friendship.*
B *But do you only want friends who agree with you on everything?*

Good reasons to end friendships
1. You don't agree on important issues.
The best ways to do it . . .

Lesson D *Online footprints*

1 Reading

A Prepare **Guess the meanings of *online footprint* and *digital dirt.* Then scan the article and find the explanations.**

B Read for main ideas **Read the article. What examples of digital dirt can you find?**

Future college students and employees, beware!

Clean up that digital dirt – now!

When student-teacher Ms. S. posted a photo from a party on the wall of her social networking site, she had no idea of the consequences. Just weeks away from obtaining a teaching degree, Ms. S.'s diploma was withheld after school administrators viewed the photo and accused her of promoting underage drinking – a charge that she denied. Her case is not an isolated one. Increasingly, employees are being fired from their jobs and students are having their college applications rejected because of "digital dirt," or inappropriate online content.

These cases highlight the need to be careful about the type of content you post online. Each time you post a photo or comment, or write a profile online, you create an image, or "online footprint," of yourself that is difficult to erase. If you think your friends are the only ones checking your profile, think again. It's increasingly common for colleges and employers to look closely at the online pictures and profiles of actual and prospective students and employees. A survey conducted by ExecuNet reported that 83 percent of job recruiters regularly use Internet searches to find out more about candidates. Nearly half said they will reject candidates based on the "digital dirt" they find.

How can you still have fun online without making a bad impression on future college admissions officers and employers? Here are five basic steps you can follow.

1. **Check what's online already.** Type your name into several search engines to see your digital footprint. Then check all of your privacy settings, and remove anything you don't want others to see. If you have "friends" who are always posting off-color jokes or rude comments about you on your wall, then block their comments.
2. **Avoid writing anything you might regret later.** Don't badmouth a current or previous employer online. The same applies to teachers, professors, classmates, or co-workers.
3. **Create a positive online image.** The Internet is the perfect place to showcase your talents and skills. Use a blog or website to promote your work, research, and interests.
4. **Use a professional email address.** An employer or a college admissions officer is more likely to contact annsmith@cup.com than smoothiefan@cup.com.
5. **Join online groups selectively.** Instead of joining groups and campaigns with names like "Sleeping in class," connect to a professional organization. When it comes time to apply for a job or place in college, you'll be glad you did.

Reading tip

Writers often begin an article with an example to illustrate their argument.

C Check your understanding **Are the sentences true (T) or false (F)? Write T or F. Correct the false sentences.**

1. Ms. S. was unable to graduate from college. _____
2. Her school said she was encouraging young people to drink. _____
3. It's becoming more common for employers to check people out online. _____
4. Eighty-three percent of job recruiters reject candidates with "digital dirt." _____
5. The article recommends "unfriending" people who post rude comments. _____
6. The article suggests that you shouldn't join social network campaigns. _____

About you | **D** React Pair work **What do you think of Ms. S.'s story? Have you heard of similar cases? Which advice in the article do you intend to follow?**

2 Focus on vocabulary Formal verbs

A **Find the verbs in bold below in the article. Match the two parts of the sentences to find the meanings. Write the letters a–g.**

1. If you **obtain** something, you _____
2. If you **withhold** something (**from** someone), you _____
3. If people **accuse** you **of (doing)** something, they _____
4. If you **promote** something, you _____
5. If you **deny (doing)** something, you _____
6. If employers **reject** a job applicant, they _____
7. If you **regret (doing)** something, you _____

a. say it is a good thing.
b. say you didn't do it.
c. don't want that person.
d. are sorry that you did it.
e. keep it and don't give it to that person.
f. say you did something bad or wrong.
g. get or achieve it.

B Pair work **Take turns using the verbs above to ask questions about Ms. S.'s story.**

"What happened before Ms. S. obtained her teaching degree?"

3 Listening and speaking But is it fair?

A Pair work **Read the question below. How many reasons can you think of to support a "yes" and a "no" answer? Make two lists.**

Today's online debate: Is it fair for employers to check out job applicants online?

B CD 1.14 **Listen to two people debate the question above. Who answers, "Yes, it's fair" and "No, it's not fair" to the question? Which of the reasons in your lists did they use?**

Rosa says __________

Daniel says __________

C CD 1.15 **Listen again and write the two missing words in each sentence.**

1. a. On the one hand, Rosa believes that what you do online shows your ________________.
   b. On the other hand, Daniel argues that your online profile is ________________.
2. a. Rosa says online profiles tell you what you won't see in ________________.
   b. Daniel thinks social networking sites don't tell you what a person is like ________________.
3. a. Rosa argues that it's ________________ to recruit and train new staff.
   b. Daniel believes that everyone has a right to ________________ in his or her free time.
4. a. Rosa says companies want people who will fit in and ________________ with other people.
   b. Daniel argues that people behave in a different way ________________.

About you

D Class debate **Prepare a response to the debate question with a partner, and then present your arguments to the class. How many people answer "yes"? How many answer "no"?**

Writing *Making judgments*

In this lesson, you . . .

- plan an argument.
- contrast ideas.
- avoid errors with *whereas.*

Task **Write a script for an online debate.**

Should employers judge applicants by their online profiles?

A Brainstorm **Read the question above. Write three reasons to answer "yes" and three reasons to answer "no."**

B Look at a model **Read the debate script. Circle three more expressions that contrast ideas.**

> Many employers check the Internet for information about job applicants. However, this is not a fair way to judge a person. On the one hand, employers need people who will fit into the company. An online profile gives information that employers will not see on a résumé – for example, if the person is aggressive or has extreme views. On the other hand, an online profile is for friends, whereas a résumé is for employers. A résumé provides the most relevant details about qualifications and work experience. An online profile may contain information that employers should not use to judge an applicant, such as age or religion. In conclusion, while there are good reasons to check an applicant's online profile, it is not a professional document. For this reason, it is not fair, in my opinion, to judge candidates by their personal online profiles.

C Focus on language **Read the grammar chart. Then use your ideas from Exercise A to complete the sentences below.**

Contrast ideas in writing

On the one hand, *employers need workers who will fit into the company.*
On the other hand, *an online profile is for friends.*

A résumé is for employers. ***However,*** *an online profile is for friends.*
A résumé is for employers, ***while/whereas/but*** *an online profile is for friends.*
While *there are reasons to check an online profile, it is not fair to do this.*

Writing vs. Conversation

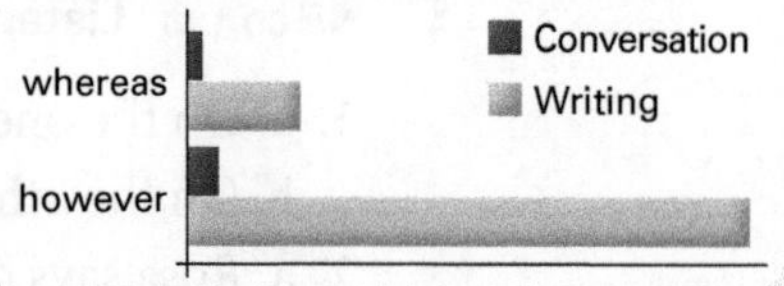

1. Introduction: *Many employers* ___________ *. Some people think* ___________ *. However,* ___________ .
2. Say why it is fair: *On the one hand, an online profile* ___________ *, whereas a résumé* ___________ .
3. Say why it is not fair: *On the other hand, an online profile* ___________ .
4. Conclusion: *In conclusion, while* ___________ *. In my opinion,* ___________ .

D Write and check **Now write your own script for the debate. Then check for errors.**

Common errors

Do not start a sentence with *Whereas* to contrast ideas with a previous sentence.
An online profile is for friends. ***However,*** *a résumé is for employers.* (NOT ~~*Whereas*~~ . . .)

Vocabulary notebook *The right choice!*

Learning tip **Formal or informal?**

When you learn informal vocabulary, write down a more formal equivalent. Don't use informal words in formal writing.

weird (informal) = odd, strange, or eccentric
touchy (informal) = sensitive, easily upset

Dictionary tip

Dictionaries often label extremely informal words as *inf(ormal), slang, colloqu(ial), rude, or taboo.*

A **Match the spoken sentences on the left with the more formal written sentences on the right.**

One of my classmates is . . .

1. a bit of a pain.
2. very chatty.
3. pretty pushy.
4. kind of touchy.
5. really weird.
6. laid-back

a. He's talkative.
b. She's sensitive.
c. She can be annoying.
d. He's very eccentric.
e. She's very relaxed about things.
f. He's very aggressive.

B **Think of three people you know. Describe each person informally and more formally.**

Person	Informal	More formal
1. ________	"________________________"	________________________
2. ________	"________________________"	________________________
3. ________	"________________________"	________________________

C **Word builder** **Find the meanings of the verbs below. Match the informal and more formal verbs. Then use each verb to say and write something true about people you know.**

Informal

badmouth   bug   chill out (with)
get a kick out of (doing)   hang out (with)

More formal

annoy   criticize   enjoy (doing)
relax (with)   socialize (with)

One guy in my class is always <u>badmouthing</u> other people.

One of my classmates is always <u>criticizing</u> other people.

brainy = intelligent

On your own

Make a dictionary of informal expressions. Write down an informal word or expression and a more formal synonym that you can use in writing or formal speech.

Unit 2

The media

In Unit 2, you . . .

- talk about the influence of the media and celebrities.
- add information with relative clauses.
- link ideas with *that* clauses.
- make comments with *which* clauses.
- use *You know what . . . ?* to introduce what you say.

Lesson A *Celebrity culture*

1 Grammar in context

A **Who are the most popular celebrities in the news? Why are they famous? How do people follow the news about them?**

B CD 1.16 **Listen to the podcast. Why is it normal to be interested in celebrities?**

ONE-MINUTE PODCASTS

Celebrity obsession is normal!

Everywhere we look these days, we see images of celebrities. Celebrity magazines, which outnumber news magazines, are on every newsstand. We love to read about the people that celebrities date, the clothes they wear, and especially their problems, which the media will often invent. Then there's reality TV. Millions of viewers avidly follow reality and talent shows, which make ordinary people into instant celebrities. There are even shows that pay for plastic surgery, so people can look like their favorite celebrity. So, why *are* we so obsessed?

Well, there's a simple scientific reason for it, which might make you feel better about your own interest in celebrity gossip. Psychologists say it's natural for us to talk about or imitate the people who are the most successful in our society. In ancient times, people gossiped about kings and leaders, who were the celebrities of their day. Nowadays, it's actors, musicians, or athletes. And with TV and the Internet, they come right into our homes, which almost makes them part of the family.

So our obsession with celebrity is perfectly normal, which is reassuring – don't you think?

About you

C Pair work **Answer the questions about the podcast. Then give your own view and add more information on each answer.**

1. Which are more popular – celebrity magazines or news magazines?
2. Why can't we always believe celebrity gossip?
3. What do some people do to look like their favorite celebrities?
4. Why are celebrities so familiar to us?

2 Grammar Adding information

Figure it out

A Check (✔) the sentence that has a complete meaning if you remove the words in bold. Then read the grammar chart.

1. We love to read about celebrities' problems, **which the media will often invent.** ☐
2. There are even shows **that pay for plastic surgery.** ☐

Defining and non-defining relative clauses

Grammar extra See page 146.

Defining relative clauses define, identify, or give essential information about a noun.
There are shows ***that/which pay for plastic surgery****.*
*We love to read about the people (****who/that****)* ***celebrities date*** *and the clothes (****that****)* ***they wear****.*

Non-defining relative clauses give extra information about a noun.
They do not begin with *that*. Notice the use of commas.
Celebrity magazines, ***which outnumber news magazines****, are everywhere.*
It's natural to talk about celebrities, ***who we see as successful people****.*

A *which* clause can add information or a comment to the clause before it.
This obsession is normal, ***which is reassuring****.*
Celebrities come into our homes, ***which almost makes them family****.*

In conversation . . .

That is more common than *which* in defining relative clauses.
Non-defining and *which* clauses often give opinions as well as information.

Common errors

Do not use *which* for people, or *what* in relative clauses.

B Complete the interview extracts with *who, that,* or *which*. If you can leave them out, write parentheses ( ) around them. Sometimes there is more than one correct answer.

1. ***Miki*** I like to read about the problems (that) celebrities are having, ________ makes me feel better about *my* problems. I don't want to know all the details of their marriages, ________ should be private, but . . . just a few things.
2. ***Tariq*** I'm interested in celebrities ________ can do other things. For example, there's Natalie Portman, ________'s a scientist. She's published in journals, ________ is interesting.
3. ***Miguel*** Well, I'll occasionally read the gossip in magazines, ________ is probably all untrue anyway. It's a distraction from work, ________ I think we all need. And it gives me something to talk about with my co-worker Jo, ________'s really into celebrity gossip and stuff.
4. ***Salwa*** Actually, I'm not interested in celebrities, ________ I feel set a bad example. You know, they often think they can do anything just because they're famous, ________ is ridiculous, really.

3 Viewpoint Who's into celebrity gossip?

Class activity **Ask your classmates the questions. Are you a celebrity-obsessed class?**

- Are you interested in celebrities? If so, what interests you about them?
- How closely do you follow celebrity gossip? Which celebrities are in the news at the moment?
- What other celebrity gossip have you heard about in the last year?

"I'm interested in the clothes that celebrities wear. I mean, they wear some weird things, which is always fun."

In conversation . . .

Use *I mean, . . .* to repeat your ideas or say more.

4 Speaking naturally *which* clauses See page 138.

Lesson B *The impact of TV*

1 Vocabulary in context

A CD 1.19 **Read the article. Which research did you already know?**

The problem with TV

Young people tune into TV for over four and a half hours every single day. That's an **increase in** TV viewing **of** 40 minutes a day compared to a few years ago. But it's not surprising that we're watching more TV. With all the latest technology, TV is now viewed online, on mobile devices such as phones and tablets, or on digital video recorders (DVRs). What's clear is that TV is central to our lives. But what kind of **impact** does it have **on** us?

1 Language development There is a lot of **research on** TV and its effects on children. What is most disturbing is that TV may have a negative **effect on** children's language development. While the results of studies vary, the opinion of most experts is that children under two should not watch TV.

2 Obesity An average teenager sees 6,000 food commercials a year, and most are **advertisements for** fast foods, candy, and sugary cereals. It is also likely that increased TV-viewing time contributes to inactivity. Experts claim that these are two of the main **reasons for** the **rise in** obesity among young people.

3 Literacy One **problem with** TV is that it reduces the time that students spend reading. Research shows that there is a direct **link between** reading and good test scores, and it's possible that TV viewing is one **cause of** poor test results.

4 Social skills There is also some **concern about** TV and its **influence on** behavior. In one survey, teachers complained that some shows encourage their students to behave badly. Other reports suggest that there is a **relationship between** watching too much TV and bullying.

B **Complete the questions with prepositions. Use the article to help you. Then ask and answer the questions with a partner.**

1. What's one reason ________ the increase ________ TV viewing over the last few years?
2. What does the article say about the effects of TV ________ children under two?
3. What foods are most food advertisements ________? Is there a problem ________ this?
4. What's another cause ________ the rise ________ obesity levels among young people?
5. What's the link ________ watching TV and reading? Why is there concern ________ this?
6. What impact does TV have ________ students' behavior?

Word sort

C **Which nouns in the article are followed by these prepositions? Write them in the chart. Some nouns take more than one preposition.**

________ about	________ between ________	________ for ________	increase in ________
________ of ________	________ on ________ ________ ________	________ with	

Vocabulary notebook

See page 29.

2 Grammar Linking ideas

Figure it out

A Rewrite each pair of sentences as one sentence. Use the article on page 22 to help you. Then read the grammar chart.

1. Children under two should not watch TV. This is the opinion of most experts.
2. We're watching more TV. It's not surprising.
3. TV is central to our lives. It's clear.
4. There is a direct link between reading and good test scores. Research shows this link.

that clauses

Grammar extra See page 147.

You can use a *that* clause after these structures. In conversation people often leave out the word *that.*

noun + *be*	*One problem with TV is* ***(that) it reduces students' reading time.***
be + adjective	*It's clear* ***(that) TV viewing contributes to inactivity.***
What's + adjective + *be*	*What's disturbing is* ***(that) TV may have an effect on language development.***
verbs, e.g., *know, think, say, show*	*Experts claim* ***(that) watching TV is one cause of obesity.***

In conversation . . .

Common expressions with *that* clauses:
The thing / problem / point is that . . .
What I'm saying is that . . .
My feeling / opinion is that . . .

B Rewrite the sentences using a *that* clause. Start with the words given, and add a verb when necessary.

1. People who watch TV spend more on consumer goods. *Experts . . .*
2. The majority of families have TV on during mealtimes. *It's disturbing . . .*
3. Most people multitask and do other things while watching TV. *What's interesting . . .*
4. Young people who watch a lot of TV are not very happy with their lives. *One recent study . . .*
5. It's not good for anyone to have a TV in the bedroom. *My feeling . . .*
6. TV is a good thing because there are lots of good educational programs. *My opinion . . .*
7. There are too many commercials and not enough good shows. *The problem with TV . . .*
8. Children are watching so much TV these days. *Teachers are concerned . . .*

About you

C Pair work **Discuss your reactions to the sentences in Exercise B.**

"I'm not surprised that there's a link between spending and watching TV. What I'm saying is that . . ."

3 Listening and speaking It's really interesting that . . .

A CD 1.20 Listen. Five people are reacting to information from the article on page 22. Which topic does each person talk about? Write the letters a, b, c, or d.

1. Maggie ____
2. Howard ____
3. Daniela ____
4. Isabel ____
5. Tony ____

a. Language development
b. Obesity
c. Literacy
d. Social skills

B CD 1.21 Listen again. Write the alternative opinion each person gives.

1. Maggie says one good thing about TV is that . . .

About you

C Pair work **Discuss your sentences in Exercise B. Do you agree with the points each person makes?**

"I think Maggie is right. What's interesting is that people never talk about how good TV can be."

Lesson C *You know what gets me?*

1 Conversation strategy Adding comments

A **How often do you watch online video clips? What different kinds of clips are there? Do you watch movies online, too?**

B CD 1.22 **Listen. What does Anna think about video clips? How about Pedro?**

Anna Did you see that video clip I emailed you?

Pedro Um, no. I don't generally tend to watch them, which is unusual, I guess. What was it?

Anna Oh, it's a couple of talking cats. It's hilarious.

Pedro Yeah? I don't mind the funny ones. You know what I don't like? People do really dangerous things and video it – like riding bikes off walls.

Anna Which is stupid, I know.

Pedro You know what gets me, too? Some of the home videos people post. They're so boring.

Anna That's true. But you know what's amazing? The number of hits they can get. I mean, they get millions.

Pedro Which is incredible. I just don't get it.

C **Notice** how Anna and Pedro use relative clauses with *which* to comment on their own and each other's statements. Find more examples in the conversation.

> ***"People do really dangerous things and video it . . ."***
> ***"Which is stupid, I know."***

D CD 1.23 **Complete the conversations with the comments in the box. Then listen and check. Practice with a partner.**

1. *A* What kinds of video clips do you tend to watch?
   B Mostly music. I subscribe to a few websites, ________________ .
2. *A* Do you ever watch those video debates on news sites?
   B Yeah, they're good. People have very different views on things.
   A ________________. I like to hear different opinions – it makes you think.
3. *A* Do you ever upload your own videos online?
   B My brother does. He'll video anything – even the wall – ________________ .
4. *A* Do you email video clips to your friends all the time?
   B No. It's a pain. I have a friend who's *always* sending clips, ________________ . I'll only send one if it's really interesting or funny.
   A ________________ .

a. which is kind of weird
b. which is a great way to find new bands
c. Which is interesting
d. Which is fine
e. which is really annoying

About you

E **Pair work** **Ask the questions in Exercise D, and give your own answers. Add comments with *which* . . . where possible.**

2 Strategy plus *You know what . . . ?*

CD 1.24 You can use ***You know what*** . . . ? to introduce a comment on what you are going to say.

You know what*'s amazing?*
You know what *gets me?*
You know what *I don't like?*

A Circle the best option to complete the *You know what . . . ?* expression. Compare with a partner.

1. You know what **interests me / I hate**? We like to watch people's home videos – why is that?
2. You know what's **amazing / so nice**? People waste so much time watching this stuff.
3. You know what**'s bad / I like**? Anyone can be creative and make a video to upload.
4. You know what**'s great / gets me**? People upload videos of their friends without permission.
5. You know what **scares me / I love**? I might be on an embarrassing video and not know.
6. You know what's **fun / annoying**? Some of the ads. They can be hilarious.

About you

B Pair work **Start conversations with six of the *You know what* . . . ? expressions in Exercise A. Do you agree with each other's views?**

A You know what I hate? All those advertisements that come on before the videos.
B I know. They can be annoying. But they're not before every video.

3 Strategies Watching movies

A Complete the *You know what . . . ?* expressions with your own ideas, and circle the best *which* . . . comments. Then practice the conversations with a partner.

1. *A* It's good that you can watch movie trailers online before you see a movie.
   B But you know what ________________ ? The trailers always look exciting. But then, when you see the movie, it's often not that good, which is **fun / a pain**.
2. *A* We usually watch movies on DVD. But you know what ________________ ? They often get stuck – like right at the best part . . .
   B Which is really **annoying / nice**. The problem is they get scratched.
3. *A* You know what ________________ ? Even though you can watch movies online and everything, the research shows that people still like to go to movie theaters.
   B Which **is terrible / isn't surprising**, really. It's more fun to watch on a big screen.
4. *A* I hate it when people tell you how a movie ends before you watch it.
   B Yeah. But you know what ________________ ? When people tell you every detail about a movie they've just seen, which is just so **exciting / boring**.

About you

B Class activity **Prepare answers to the questions. Give reasons. Then survey the class. What is the consensus?**

- What do you think about online movies and videos?
- Do you have any concerns about their content?
- What are the good things about them? What are the problems?

A Well, one problem with some of the music videos is that they can be offensive.
B I agree. You know what gets me? All that bad language, which is just awful.

Lesson D *A bad influence?*

1 Reading

A Prepare Which of these statements about violence in the media do you agree with?

1. It can make people aggressive.
2. It's just harmless entertainment.
3. It's harmful to children.
4. It should be banned.

B Understanding viewpoints Read the article. Which of the statements in Exercise A would the writer agree with? Find reasons for your answers in the article.

NOT JUST A GAME

1 Whether we like it or not, violence is part of all mass media. It's on TV and the Internet, in movies, music, and the video games people play. What is most disturbing perhaps is that it's not just in adult entertainment. On a typical Saturday morning, children's television shows up to 25 acts of violence per hour, which means that by the age of 18, the average person has witnessed around 200,000 violent acts. [**1** ______]

2 What kind of impact does this have on young people? Over 25 years ago, psychologists found that elementary-school children who watched many hours of violence on television had more aggressive behavior as teenagers. In recent years, however, researchers have turned their attention to the problem of violence in video games, which are now a more popular form of entertainment than movies.

3 One disturbing trend in video-game design is the number of games that include extreme violence and killing. Critics of video games are concerned about the impact that these types of video games can have, especially on young people. Violent games are often blamed for aggressive behavior on school playgrounds and, in extreme cases, for the rise in school shootings.

4 However, are violent video games the cause of violent behavior? [**2** ______]

5 Psychologists claim that there *is* evidence to suggest that playing violent video games really does make people feel, think, and behave more aggressively. [**3** ______] The research also suggests that video games have a greater influence than television because they are interactive and players identify with and take on the role of the killers in the games.

6 There *are* games that reward players for positive, pro-social behaviors such as cooperating or sharing. However, children tend to prefer games that require them to be aggressive, violent, or competitive in order to win. One point that critics of violent video games make is that these games are regularly used as part of military training, where the aim is to desensitize the players to killing. The same seems to be happening to young people, they say.

7 [**4** ______] In one study, 80 percent of junior high school students said they were familiar with a particular violent computer game, but fewer than 5 percent of parents had even heard of it, which proves how little parents are engaging with this complex issue.

8 Isn't it time for us all to take more interest in the effect that media violence has on us, and do something about it?

Reading tip

Writers often ask a question and then answer it to build their argument. (See paragraphs 2 and 4.)

C Read for detail Where do these sentences fit in the article? Write the correct letters in the spaces. There is one extra sentence.

a. Furthermore, children who enjoy aggressive video and computer games show less pro-social behavior, such as helping people.
b. Parents need to be more aware of the violent games that their children are playing.
c. Parents of teenagers are also concerned about violent music lyrics.
d. By the age of 11, a U.S. child will typically have seen 8,000 murders on TV.
e. The short answer seems to be "yes."

2 Focus on vocabulary Formal expressions

A Find more formal ways in the article of expressing the underlined ideas. Write the number of words indicated.

turned their attention to

1. Researchers have started looking at video games. (4 words: para. 2)
2. Some games have really bad violence and killing. (1 word: para. 3)
3. People who don't like video games say they are harmful. (2 words: para. 3)
4. Players think they are like the characters in the games. (2 words: para. 5)
5. Children knew about games that their parents hadn't heard of. (3 words: para. 7)
6. Violence in video games is a very difficult subject. (2 words: para. 7)

About you

B Pair work **What new facts did you learn from the article? How did the information affect your views on violence in the media? Discuss with a partner.**

"I think it's interesting that the average person sees 200,000 violent acts by the age of 18. That has to have an effect on you . . ."

3 Listening and speaking They're just games!

A CD 1.25 **Listen to part of a lecture about violence and the media. Choose the best phrase to complete the summary of the speaker's argument.**

There ______________ between violence in the media and crime.

a. is a clear link   b. is no proof of a link   c. are a number of links

B CD 1.26 **Listen again. Circle the correct option to complete the information about the lecture.**

1. The speaker **agrees / does not agree** that violent entertainment makes people aggressive.
2. Over the last 25 years, there has been a **rise / drop** in violent youth crime.
3. Around 90 percent of boys and **14 / 40** percent of girls play video games.
4. He says that people **can / can't** tell the difference between fact and fiction.
5. He claims that there is **some / no** evidence that games turn people into killers.

About you

C Group work **Discuss the questions. Give reasons for your answers.**

1. Were you surprised by anything the speaker said? What did you find most interesting?
2. Do you think there is too much violence in the media?
3. Do you know people who enjoy violent entertainment? Do they tend to be more aggressive?
4. Should we have the right to choose what we watch and play?
5. Is it possible to stop children from seeing extreme violence? If so, how?

Writing *Should it be banned?*

In this lesson, you . . .

- use topic sentences.
- list ideas.
- avoid errors with listing expressions.

Task **Write a paragraph.**

Songs with violent lyrics make people more violent and should be banned. Do you agree or disagree?

A **Look at a model** **Read the paragraph from an essay. Check (✓) the two good topic sentences below, and choose one to write in the space.**

While many people feel that music with violent lyrics should be banned, we need to look closely at this argument. ______________________ First, the main problem with banning this music is that it becomes more attractive, especially to young people. People who did not listen to it before might become interested in it, which may make it even more popular. Second, there is no proof that this music makes people violent. A lot of people enjoy it, which does not mean that they are violent people. Finally, people can find all kinds of music on the Internet, which means that a ban will not work.

Topic sentences

A topic sentence gives the main idea or topic of a paragraph. The other sentences should support the main idea.

- ☐ a. Music is something that everyone loves.
- ☐ b. I like this type of music.
- ☐ c. It is unlikely that a ban will work for several reasons.
- ☐ d. This music does not make people more violent.
- ☐ e. There are at least three problems with banning this type of music.

B **Focus on language** **Circle two more expressions in the paragraph in Exercise A that organize the ideas. Then read the grammar chart.**

Listing ideas in writing

There are at least three problems with banning this music.
First, *it may become more attractive to young people.*
Second, . . . ***Third, . . .*** ***Finally, / Lastly,*** *people can find all kinds of music on the Internet.*

Writing vs. Conversation

- *First, Second, Finally,* and *Lastly* are much more common in writing.
- *First of all* is more common in conversation.

C **Brainstorm** **What's your answer to the essay question? Think of three reasons to support your answer. Complete the sentences with your ideas. Then compare with a partner.**

1. Say if you agree or disagree: *I agree/disagree with the statement that* ______________________
2. Give reason 1: *First,* ______________________
3. Give reason 2: *Second,* ______________________
4. Give reason 3: *Finally,* ______________________

D **Write and check** **Now write a paragraph that gives your answer to the essay question and the reasons for it. Include a clear topic sentence. Then check for errors.**

Common errors

Use *First* and *Lastly* when you list ideas.
There are two reasons for this.
First*, this music is . . .* (NOT ~~*At first, . . .*~~)
Lastly*, the Internet has . . .* (NOT ~~*At last, . . .*~~)

Vocabulary notebook *What an effect!*

Learning tip Nouns and prepositions

When you write down a new noun, find out what prepositions (if any) are used with it. Write a short sentence and complete it with two or more ideas.

concern about
There is concern about — obesity. / advertising. / television.

A Complete the notes and sentences with prepositions. Then add another idea that could replace the bold words in each sentence.

1. advertisement for ______ There are a lot of advertisements for ______ **fast food** on television. (children's toys)
2. cause ______ One cause ______ low test scores may be **TV viewing**.
3. concern ______ There is a lot of concern ______ **childhood obesity**.
4. effect ______ Advertising may have an effect ______ **children's diets**.
5. influence ______ TV has a big influence ______ **children's behavior**.
6. impact ______ Television has an impact ______ **young children**.
7. link ______ There is a link ______ TV viewing and **language development**.
8. problem ______ One problem ______ television is **the number of commercials**.
9. relationship ______ There's a relationship ______ reading and **test scores**.
10. reason ______ What are the reasons ______ **obesity**?
11. research ______ The research ______ **TV viewing** is very clear.
12. rise ______ There has been a rise ______ **bullying in schools**.

B Word builder Find out which prepositions you can use with these nouns, and complete the sentences. Then use your own ideas to write one more sentence for each noun + preposition.

1. attitude ______ We should change our attitude ______ television and what it can offer.
2. connection ______ There seems to be a connection ______ the amount of television kids watch and their ability to pay attention.
3. information ______ We need more information ______ the effects of bullying.
4. need ______ There's a need ______ better programming on TV.

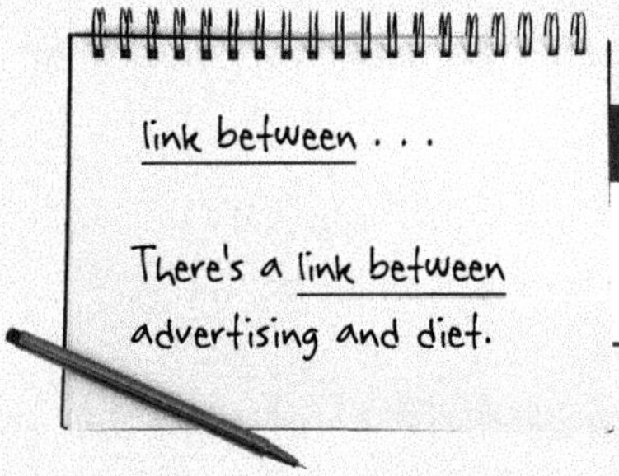

On your own

Make a flip pad of nouns and prepositions. Write a different noun on every page.

Unit 3

Stories

In Unit 3, you . . .

- talk about life lessons and experiences.
- use the past tense, the present perfect, and the past perfect.
- make comments when telling a story.
- use *(It's) no wonder . . .* to say something is not surprising.

Lesson A *Highlights*

1 Grammar in context

A **What are some typical highlights in people's lives? Make a list.**

"Well, getting into college seems to be a real highlight for a lot of people."

B CD 1.27 **Listen to the interviews. What special things has each person done?**

We interviewed people and asked,
"What are some of the highlights of your life so far?"

JANIE, 35
Vancouver, Canada: high school teacher

"Oh, I've been pretty lucky up until now. For one thing, I've traveled a lot. I lived in Italy a couple of years ago. That was amazing. Then after Italy, I went to Central America and worked with a team of volunteers. We were rebuilding homes after a major earthquake for two months. It was hard work but so rewarding. Life has definitely been interesting so far."

MARCOS, 25
Belo Horizonte, Brazil: college student

"Um, I've done some interesting things in the last few years. I started a band the year before last, though it didn't last – we broke up after six months. But it was fun. And I've been coaching a local soccer team for the last two years. That's been good. We've won most of our matches. I still haven't decided what I want to do after I graduate. I haven't thought too much about it . . . yet. But that's OK!"

JING-WEI, 25 and SHENG, 27
Beijing, China: designer and graduate student

"Well, we haven't really done anything except work over the last few years. We met when we were in college. Sheng was getting his master's, and I was studying design. Then Sheng started his PhD. Since then, he's just been concentrating on school."
"Jing-Wei got an internship at a fashion company last year. That was a big thing for her. You've been enjoying it so far, haven't you?"

About you

C Pair work **Discuss the questions about the people. Give your own opinions.**

Who . . .

1. has the most initiative?
2. works very hard?
3. makes the most out of life?
4. is doing something you'd like to do?
5. has the most exciting life?

"I think Janie has the most initiative. It's great that she did that volunteer work and . . ."

2 **Grammar** Talking about the past

Figure it out

A Find the sentences below in the interviews. Do they refer to a completed past time (C) or a past time that continues up to now (N)? Write C or N. Then read the grammar chart.

1. After Italy I went to Central America. _____
2. Life has definitely been interesting so far. _____
3. I started a band the year before last. _____
4. Since then, he's been concentrating on school. _____

The past tense vs. the present perfect

Grammar extra *See page 148.*

Use the past tense for situations and events that are part of a completed past time, not connected to now.	Use the present perfect for situations and events that are part of a past time that continues up to now.
past time *now*	*past time* ⟶ *now*
*I **lived** in Italy a few years ago.* (I'm not there now.) *The band **didn't last.** We **broke up** after six months.*	*Life **has been** interesting so far.* (It still is.) *Marcos **hasn't decided** what he wants to do yet.*

Use simple verbs for completed events or permanent situations.
*Marcos's band **broke up.*** *I**'ve been** pretty lucky.*

Use continuous verbs for background, ongoing, or temporary events or situations.
*We **were rebuilding** homes.* *He**'s been coaching** a soccer team.*

B Complete the conversations with an appropriate form of the verbs given. Sometimes more than one option may be possible. Then practice with a partner.

1. *A* Have you had any interesting opportunities in the last couple of years?
   B Um, last year I _________ (join) a gymnastics team. Since then, we _________ (compete) at several events, but so far we _________ (not win) anything.
2. *A* Have you traveled much over the last few years?
   B Well, I _________ (not go) away last year, but the year before, when I _________ (study) geography in college, we _________ (take) a trip to Alaska. That _________ (be) fun. I _________ (not travel) much since then.
3. *A* What's been the highlight of your year so far?
   B Actually, up until now, I _________ (not do) anything special because I _________ (be) so busy with school. I _________ (work) on my thesis all year, so I _________ (not have) much time for anything else. I _________ (take) a short break last weekend, though, and I _________ (go) hiking, but that's all.

About you

C Pair work **Take turns asking and answering the questions in Exercise B. Give your own answers.**

3 **Viewpoint** So far . . .

Group work **Tell your group about three highlights in your life so far. Ask your classmates questions to find out more information.**

A *One highlight for me is that I met my favorite baseball player. He was giving out baseball jerseys at a game.*

B *That's so cool. Did he sign them?*

In conversation . . .

Use expressions like these to react to people's stories.
That's so great/amazing/cool/interesting.

Lesson B *Life lessons*

1 Vocabulary in context

A Read the blog. What is the story about? Can you guess what the professor said?

http://www.cambridge.org/lorena

LIVING AND LEARNING

SEARCH THIS BLOG

HOME | LATEST POST | OTHER LIFE LESSONS | TOP POSTS

An important life lesson . . .

May 10TH 11:13:48 PM by Lorena

I've learned many things in life, but this is one lesson I learned early on. I hope it makes you think . . .

Toward the end of my last semester in college, our ethics professor gave us a test. He had told us to expect one and had warned us it would **count toward our final grade**. I had been **struggling with the class** all semester because I'd **missed** a number of **classes** and I'd **fallen behind on my work**. But by the day of the test, I had **caught up on** all **the work** and I felt pretty confident.

Sure enough, 40 minutes into the test, I had **finished** all **the questions** except the very last one: *What is the name of the woman who cleans the lecture hall?*

I thought it was a joke. I'd seen the woman many times. She was short with dark hair, in her fifties, and she'd been working in the building for at least a year. We'd even smiled at each other once or twice. But I didn't know her name because I'd never thought to ask her.

I **turned in my test** and **left the** last **question blank** – hoping I wouldn't get penalized too badly for it. But then one student **raised his hand**. He hadn't **finished the test**, either. "I'm just wondering," he said and paused. "Will it *really* **affect my grade** if I don't **complete that** last **question**?"

Our professor smiled. "Absolutely," he said. "In your careers, ______________."

I've never forgotten that lesson. I also learned that the janitor's name was Sherry.

ABOUT ME

View my complete profile

About you

B CD 1.28 **Listen to the story. Did you have a similar ending? What do you think of the professor's response?**

C Pair work **Prepare answers to the questions. Give reasons using expressions from the story. Then compare with a partner.**

1. Why was the ethics test an important one?
2. What was Lorena's experience with her ethics class?
3. What problem did she have with the test?
4. Why was she concerned that she would get penalized?
5. How did the professor answer the student who raised his hand?

Word sort

D How many expressions from the blog can you find that include these words? Add other ideas. Then take turns using each expression to ask your partner a question.

miss a class	________ a grade	________ a test
________ your work	________ your hand	________ a question (________)

Vocabulary notebook

See page 39.

"Have you ever missed a class?"

2 Grammar Sequencing events

Figure it out

A When did each event below happen: on the day of the test (D) or before the day of the test (B)? Write D or B. What do you notice about the verb forms? Then read the grammar chart.

1. The professor gave us a test. _____
2. He had told us to expect it. _____
3. I'd been struggling with the class. _____
4. I felt pretty confident. _____

The simple past, past perfect, and past perfect continuous

Grammar extra *See page 149.*

Use the simple past for two or more events that are part of the same past time period.

past event + past event *now*	past event 1 / past event 2 *He **raised** his hand and **asked** a question.*

Use the past perfect for an event that is part of a time period before another event in the past.

earlier past event *past event* *now*	earlier past event / past event *He **had told** us to expect a test. We **took** it last week.*

Use the past perfect continuous for background, ongoing, or temporary events or situations.

ongoing earlier past event *past event* *now*	ongoing earlier past event / past event *I'**d been struggling** . . ., but I **felt** confident on the day.*

In conversation . . .

People often use the past perfect to give reasons or explanations.

*I didn't know her name **because I'd never thought to ask her.***

B Complete the anecdote with the verbs given. Use one simple past and one past perfect verb in each sentence.

"Right before I _________ (move) here, I _________ (lose) my job. I _________ (not have) an interview for weeks, and I _________ (be) concerned, you know. And I _________ (think) about going back to school, but actually, I _________ (not want) to. And then out of the blue, I _________ (get) an email from an old friend that I _________ (not contact) in ages."

C Complete the rest of the anecdote with the past perfect or past perfect continuous form of the verbs given. Sometimes both are possible. Then take turns retelling the story to a partner.

"And it turned out that he _________ (start up) his own company. But he _________ (struggle) to find someone to work for him for some time, and he _________ (not found) anyone suitable. Well, actually, he _________ (hire) one woman, but she _________ (quit) after the first month because she _________ (not be able) to travel so much. Anyway, I _________ (look) for a job in sales, and he offered me the job. So, yeah, I learned it's good to keep in touch with people!"

3 Listening and speaking It just goes to show . . .

A What do these sayings mean? Check (✔) the ones you agree with.

☐ a. You can't judge a book by its cover.
☐ b. You've got to stop and smell the roses.
☐ c. Truth is stranger than fiction.
☐ d. Life's too short.

B CD 1.29 **Listen to three stories. How will each story end? Number the sayings above 1–3.**

C CD 1.30 **Listen and check your answers.**

About you

D Group work **Take turns telling about an important life lesson you've learned.**

"I've learned to think positively. In high school, I'd been applying to lots of different colleges, but . . ."

4 Speaking naturally Auxiliary verbs *See page 139.*

Lesson C *Anyway, back to my story . . .*

1 Conversation strategy Telling stories

A Look at these expressions from a conversation. What do they mean? Can you guess what the conversation is about?

picture day at school | it was a big deal | scruffy-looking | my hair was sticking up

B CD 1.33 **Listen. Why was picture day a big deal for Brad's family?**

Arnold Look at this old class photo. I mean, look at our hair!

Brad I know. You should see one of my school photos. We'd forgotten it was picture day, and looking back, picture day was a big deal in our house. My mom showed the photos to everybody and sent them out to my aunts. I hated it.

Arnold No wonder.

Brad Yeah. And she made me wear a shirt and tie. It's no wonder I hated it. But anyway, back to my story . . . so this one day I went to school as usual, which means I hadn't combed my hair and I was wearing an old T-shirt. I mean, when I think about it, I was always really scruffy-looking.

Arnold Yeah, me too. I didn't care how I looked back then.

Brad No, me neither. So anyway, where was I?

Arnold You went to school on picture day all scruffy . . .

C Notice how Brad interrupts his story to make a comment and comes back to it with expressions like these. Find examples in the conversation.

Interrupting a story:	Coming back to the story:
Looking back, . . . *When I look back, . . .* *When I think about it, . . .*	*(But/So) anyway, . . .* *Anyway, (getting) back to my story, . . .*

D CD 1.34 **Listen to more of their conversation and write the missing expressions. Then practice the conversation with a partner. Practice again, using different expressions.**

Brad . . . Oh, yeah. So there I was in the front row – with my hair sticking up and a hole in my shirt. Right next to our teacher, Mr. Gray.

Arnold Yeah? That's funny.

Brad Yeah. _______________ *(interrupt)*, he was a funny guy – nice but eccentric. He wore a bow tie and these little glasses, which he was always losing. _______________ *(back to the story)*, when we got the photos the following week, my mom took one look at them and cried.

Arnold She did? She actually cried?

Brad Oh, yeah. I mean, _______________ *(interrupt)*, picture day was the one day a year I looked good. It was a special day to her! _______________ *(back to the story)*, she took me to a photographer and had my picture taken there.

2 Strategy plus *No wonder.*

CD 1.35 You can use ***No wonder*** as a response to a comment on an experience that is not surprising.

You can also use (***It's***) ***no wonder*** (***that***) to introduce a comment.

It's no wonder *I hated it.*

In conversation . . .

People mostly say *No wonder* . . .

No wonder . . . . . ■■■■■

It's no wonder . . . ■

A Match the sentences and the responses. Write the letters a–e. Then practice with a partner.

1. French classes were my favorite. _____
2. I walked two miles to school every day. _____
3. Lunch was always hot dogs and fries. _____
4. I couldn't wait for the summer. _____
5. I always fell behind in math. I hated it! _____

a. It's no wonder that kids are overweight.
b. No wonder. It's the best time of year.
c. Me too. It's no wonder we were fit.
d. No wonder. It's no fun if you're struggling.
e. It's no wonder you're so fluent.

About you

B Pair work **Make the sentences true for you, and add a comment with *(It's) no wonder* . . .**

"French was my least favorite class. It's no wonder I can't speak a word of it."

3 Strategies Childhood stories

A Complete each anecdote with the expressions in the box. Then take turns telling the stories. Listen to your partner and make comments.

anyway	But anyway	It's no wonder	when I look back

1. "One day my teacher asked me for help. We'd been painting pictures of flowers. We painted a lot in that class. So ________________, I picked up this cup and said, 'I can put it away.' You know, ________________, I was always trying to help the teacher. I was a good kid. ________________, I had this cup, which was full of dirty paint water, and I spilled it all over her skirt. ________________ she never asked for my help again!"

But anyway, back to my story	looking back	No wonder	When I think about it

2. *A* I won first prize one time in a bicycle-safety contest. And ________________, it was really special because I'd never come first in anything. I wrote this slogan: *A five-minute check might save your neck.* ________________, I loved playing with words, even then. ________________. I was so excited – I thought the prize was a bike. But I just got a pen. I was so disappointed.

   B ________________.

About you

B Group work **Use a chart like this one to prepare a story about your childhood (e.g., a fun or scary time, or a time you got into trouble). Then take turns telling your stories.**

The story	Comments
1. I heard some noises in the yard one night.	I was a nervous kid – always scared at night.

Lesson D *Good fiction*

1 Reading

A Prepare **What good fiction have you read recently? Who are your favorite authors?**

B Read for main ideas **Read the winning entry in a short-story contest. What is Janet's problem?**

Saturday

By Susan Ingram

1 Janet couldn't remember when she'd first realized she was invisible. She supposed it had started, well, maybe it had started before, but she first noticed it when she would look into someone's eyes, say a passerby on the street, or even someone in the hallway at work when she was pushing the mail cart from office to office.

2 She had always thought it was only human. What you did as a part of a community, a part of society. When someone passes by, you look them in the eyes, smile and say hi, or hello, or how's it going?

3 Janet always did. To everyone. Of course, not everyone responded. Some people looked away. Some acted like they didn't see her, or didn't hear her. She always felt sorry for people like that. What was it like not to be able to smile and say hi? She couldn't imagine.

4 But lately, she had noticed that not only was no one saying hi back, no one was even acknowledging her. As if she weren't even there. Just as if they couldn't see her at all.

5 Then stranger things happened. One day, when she was in line at her local donut shop, the woman behind the counter waited on the guy in front of her, then looked through her and asked the girls behind her, "May I help you?"

6 She began ordering from the drive-through window. They could hear her voice, apparently, through the cheap speakers. Could see at least her truck when she pulled up to the window. They would slip her the medium half-decaf with vanilla cream and take her bills and give her change. All without making eye contact.

7 She would drive away, smiling, eyes wide, and shake her head and sip her coffee and wonder what was happening in the world.

8 This morning, a clear, hard winter morning, a Saturday, Janet pulled out of the drive-through, doubled back into the parking lot still piled high with mountains of snow, and parked. She'd been stuck in the house for three days, the office closed, her neighborhood like something from another planet.

9 She grabbed the newspaper from the seat next to her. It was the first paper she'd gotten since the day before the storm. She found it sitting in the sun on top of a six-foot mound of snow at the end of her driveway like a yellow-plastic-bagged Valentine's Day gift.

10 With her coffee and bag in one hand and the newspaper tucked under her arm, she pushed through the door of the donut shop, where she hadn't ventured in months, and made her way to a small table by the window. There were a few people at a high-top at the opposite window. A couple of workers in headsets and caps moved behind the counter. No one looked up as she crossed to her table and sat down.

11 Janet sipped at the coffee. It was hot and almost burned her tongue. She slipped the newspaper out of the plastic sleeve and spread it out on the table. A small, wrinkled man was making his way toward her, sliding a large rag mop across the already clean floor. Janet lifted her feet as he mopped under her table. He put the mop in the bucket and reached over for her newspaper, sliding it halfway off the table before Janet slapped her hand down, stopping it. The man looked puzzled and tugged again.

12 "Hello," Janet said and smiled. The man looked up into her eyes.

13 "Oh, hello," he said, smiling back. "I didn't see you."

14 "Now you do," she said. "Now you do."

Reading tip

Fiction writers often break up sentences into small parts to create interest and drama.

To everyone. All without making eye contact.

These sentences can be ungrammatical, so don't use them in your writing for school.

C Pair work **Understand and react Discuss the questions.**

- What kind of woman do you think Janet is?
- Why did Janet feel invisible?
- How do you think Janet felt on the Saturday morning after the storm?
- What do you think the restaurant worker was thinking about while he was cleaning?
- Was he rude to Janet, do you think? Do you think Janet was rude to him?

2 Focus on vocabulary Verbs

A Find the verbs in the story. Match them with their meanings. Write the letters a–h.

1. say (para. 1) _____
2. acknowledge (para. 4) _____
3. slip (para. 6) _____
4. make eye contact (para. 6) _____
5. venture (para. 10) _____
6. make (your) way (para. 11) _____
7. slap down (para. 11) _____
8. tug (para. 11) _____

a. nod or smile to show you see someone
b. move something quickly so people don't notice
c. hit with a flat hand
d. walk toward
e. for example, like
f. go somewhere risky or unpleasant
g. look at someone directly in the eye
h. pull hard

B Pair work **What can you remember about the story? Take turns retelling the story in your own words. Try to include as many details as you can.**

"It's about a woman who noticed people had been ignoring her. They didn't . . ."

3 Listening and speaking How friendly are people?

A Which statement below best describes people in your town or city? Give examples.

☐ a. People are extremely friendly.
☐ b. People are friendly if you're friendly to them.
☐ c. People are very unfriendly.
☐ d. People are polite but not that friendly.

B CD 1.36 **Listen to three students describe the people in their cities. Which statement in Exercise A summarizes what they say? Number the statements 1–3. There is one extra statement.**

C CD 1.37 **Listen again. Each person tells an anecdote to illustrate a point. Where were the people and what happened? Make notes and compare with a partner.**

About you

D Group work **Create a list of rules that would make your city a friendlier place to live.**

"Well, I think people should acknowledge other people when they come into contact with them. Like, if you get into an elevator with someone, you should at least smile."

In conversation . . .

You can use *like* to give examples.

Writing *What do you expect?*

In this lesson, you . . .

- brainstorm and then plan an article.
- use verbs to structure an article.
- avoid errors with the past perfect.

Task Write a narrative article.

Write an article for a college magazine about a time you experienced good or bad behavior.

A Look at a model **Number the paragraphs in the correct order. Find an introduction (1), background events (2), main events (3, 4), and a conclusion (5). Which verb forms are used in each part?**

____ Since then, I've often thought about that day. I know if I ever find someone's bag, I'll do the right thing.

____ I ran across the platform, but the doors of the train started to close, and in a last effort to get on the train, I threw my bag onto it. The doors slammed shut, and I stood on the platform as the train pulled slowly away. I felt so stupid. I'd just thrown my bag with my computer and wallet onto a train!

____ I remember one day, I was running to catch the subway to go to an interview. I was feeling stressed because I was late and I'd been running around all morning.

____ I looked around for help, but of course, everyone ignored me. The next day, I called the lost and found department to ask if they had my bag. They didn't. Someone had taken it.

__1__ I like to think, generally, that people are honest and that they will always do the right thing. Unfortunately, this is not always the case.

B Focus on language **Read the chart. Then complete the article below with appropriate forms of the verbs given. Sometimes more than one option may be possible.**

Verbs in narrative writing

You can use:

- the present tense to introduce your article: *I **like** to think that people **are** honest.*
- continuous forms for background events: *I **was feeling** stressed. I**'d been running** around.*
- simple past forms for main events: *I **threw** my bag onto it. The doors **slammed** shut.*
- the present perfect to link events to now: *I**'ve** often **thought** about that day.*

It __________ (be) simply good manners to hold doors open for people, but not everyone __________ (be) so considerate. One day I __________ (go) into an office building. I __________ (carry) a big box of paper, which I __________ (deliver) to a business. Suddenly, a woman who __________ (walk) behind me __________ (push) right in front of me. She __________ (open) the heavy glass door and __________ (not hold) it for me. The door __________ (slam) in my face, and I __________ (fall) backwards on the sidewalk. Since then, I __________ always __________ (make) sure that I hold doors open for people.

C Brainstorm and plan **Think of ideas for your article. Then use the headings to help you plan it.**

1. Introduction: ______________________________
2. Background events: ______________________________
3. Main events: ______________________________
4. Conclusion / link to now: ______________________________

Common errors

The past perfect is *had* + a past participle. Do not use *had* + a simple past form of the verb.

*I**'d** just **thrown** my bag onto a train.* (NOT *I'd just ~~threw~~ . . .*)

D Write and check **Write your article. Then check for errors.**

Vocabulary notebook *Catch up!*

Learning tip **Writing definitions**

When you learn a new expression, write a definition to help you remember it.

If you struggle with a class, you have a difficult time with it (for example., because the work is hard or there's too much to do).

A Complete the definitions with a correct form of the expressions in the box.

affect your grade	count toward your final grade	leave a question blank
catch up on your work	fall behind on your work	✓ raise your hand

1. If you ____raise your hand____, you put it in the air to get someone's attention – for example, when you want to ask a question in class.
2. If you ________________, you can't do all the things you are supposed to do on time.
3. If you ________________, you don't write an answer to it.
4. If tests or assignments ________________, they are part of your final score.
5. If assignments ________________, they can make a difference to your grade.
6. If you ________________, you do all the work on your desk that you had to do or that is late.

B Now write definitions for these expressions.

1. miss a class ________________
2. complete a question ________________
3. turn in a test ________________
4. finish a test ________________

C Word builder Find the meanings of the expressions in the box, and write definitions for them.

attend a class   drop a class   fail a class   hand in an assignment   repeat a class/grade

1. ________________
2. ________________
3. ________________
4. ________________
5. ________________

We *catch up* on . . .

The things people talk about *catching up on* most are: *sleep, reading, correspondence, paperwork.*

On your own

What can you do to improve your work for your classes? Make a list in English in the front of your notebook. Review the list in a week. Are you sticking to the challenges?

Checkpoint 1 *Units 1–3*

1 TV time

A Complete the conversations with a correct form of the verbs given. Then practice in pairs.

1. *Kamal* Do you ever eat dinner in front of the TV?
   Lynn Not really. Though on Friday nights, we tend to watch (tend / watch) a movie and often we ________ (will / order) a pizza or something. But we ________ (tend / sit) at the table. And when we ________ (have) dinner, you know, we ________ (talk) about our day and things.
   Kamal Which ________ (be) nice. My son ________ always ________ (text) – even at the table! He ________ (play) around with his phone all through dinner, so I guess we ________ (not talk) much as a family.
2. *Diego* What do you think about all the TV commercials for fast-food places?
   Nagwa Well, there are way too many. But you know what ________ (get) me? The fast-food places ________ always ________ (advertise) toys, too, which ________ (be) annoying because the kids want to eat there then.
   Diego I know. My kids ________ constantly ________ (complain) because I ________ (not take) them to fast-food places. But my wife ________ (not want) them to eat fast food, so . . .
3. *Colin* Do you watch a lot of TV?
   Minh Um, not really. But my brother ________ (live) in front of the TV. He even ________ (do) his homework when he ________ (watch) TV, which I'm sure ________ (have) an effect on his grades.

About you

B Pair work **Discuss the questions in Exercise A. Comment on your partner's answers using *which* clauses.**

A *We never have the TV on during dinner. We tend to listen to music.*
B *Which is always nice. We listen to the radio when we're having dinner.*

2 What are they like?

A Complete the sentences with *who, that,* or *which*. If you can leave them out, write parentheses ( ) around them. Sometimes there is more than one correct answer.

1. My best friend has a great sense of humor, which is something I like a lot.
2. My sister, ________ is really talkative, is very open-minded.
3. I like people ________ are relaxed, but my boss, ________ is very sweet, is just too laid-back.
4. The most interesting person ________ I know is my Uncle Rick, ________ is a bit eccentric.
5. My dad's a sensitive guy, ________ makes him a little touchy – especially with people ________ are pushy.

About you

B Pair work **Take turns describing people you know. Ask your partner checking or information questions with *So, And,* or *But*.**

A *My sister's a really thoughtful person. She always remembers everyone's birthday.*
B *So she sends a lot of cards?* OR *But how does she remember?*

3 It has an influence on you

Pair work **Write a preposition for each noun. Then use each phrase in a sentence.**

1. advertisement for 3. effect ____ 5. increase / rise ____ 7. problem ____ 9. relationship ____
2. cause ____ 4. impact ____ 6. link ____ 8. reason ____ 10. research ____

"I saw an advertisement today for those new smart phones."

4 At school

About you

Complete the sentences with the expressions in the box. Use the correct form of the verbs. Then use each expression in a true sentence.

affect my grades	count toward	leave a lot of questions blank	not raise my hand	turn in my test paper
catch up on	fall behind on	✓ miss a class	struggle with	

1. I missed a class last week, which is too bad. The teacher reviewed stuff for the final exam.
2. I'm not doing very well in school. I've been ________ my classes. Two assignments that ________ my final grade are late. I really need to ________ my work.
3. I hate asking questions in class. I mean, I ________ once this semester!
4. I haven't been studying enough recently, and I know it's been ________.
5. Math was really hard for me last semester. I'd been ________ the class all year, actually. But on the final exam, I ________. I couldn't do them. So I just ________ and left.

Actually, I've been going to all my classes this semester. I haven't missed one class.

5 Problem solved!

A Complete the story with the verbs given. Use the simple past, past perfect, or past perfect continuous. Sometimes more than one form may be possible.

"When I was 17, I wanted (want) to go to college, but I ________ (not finish) high school. I ________ (need) one more credit, so I ________ (decide) to take art history at night school. It was great. ☐ I ________ always ________ (like) art – even before I took that course. ☐ the teacher________ (be) pretty cool. She ________ (play) classical music in class. ☐ I guess that's when I ________ (learn) to love Mozart. ☐ she ________ (ask) us to write an essay on a famous artist, so I ________ (choose) Vincent van Gogh. I ________ (not start) my essay until the night before it was due because I ________ (work) at my uncle's store all semester. I sat down to write, but I ________ (leave) all my art books at work. I only ________ (have) a book of van Gogh's letters to his brother, Theo. Also, I ________ (forgot) to buy paper. So for my essay, I ________ (write) letters from Theo to Vincent on my mother's fancy writing paper! My teacher ________ (love) it. ☐ I leave things till the last minute. It often works out!"

B Add these expressions to the story. Write the numbers 1–5 in the boxes. There may be more than one correct answer. Then take turns telling the story with a partner.

1. When I think about it,
2. It's no wonder that
3. Looking back,
4. Anyway, getting back to my story,
5. So anyway,

About you

C Pair work **Was it fair that the writer got a good grade? Is it OK to leave things to the last minute? Is it good to work *and* study? Discuss your answers using the expressions below.**

My feeling is that . . .	What's interesting is that . . .	I think that . . .
It's possible that . . .	What I'm saying is that . . .	You know what I think?

Unit 4

Working lives

In Unit 4, you . . .

- talk about work and finding a job.
- use countable and uncountable nouns.
- generalize and specify with articles.
- use *-ly* adverbs to express your attitude.
- use *As a matter of fact* and *In fact* to give or correct information.

Lesson A *Stand out from the crowd!*

1 Vocabulary in context

A CD 2.02 **What do you think employers look for in job applicants? Make a list. Then read the article. Which of your ideas are mentioned?**

WHAT EMPLOYERS WANT . . .

AND OUR ADVICE!

In today's job market, candidates **face** stiff **competition**. The evidence suggests that applicants who do their homework on an employer before they **submit an application** stand out from the crowd. Recent research shows what employers look for in new hires. Information like this is often the key to landing your dream job.

EMPLOYERS OFTEN LOOK FOR . . .

1. PEOPLE WHO HAVE LONG-TERM POTENTIAL In interviews, **show interest** in moving ahead in your career. Ask about the career paths of other employees and possible promotions.

2. EVIDENCE YOU CAN WORK WELL WITH OTHERS Give an example of how you collaborated with others on a project to **make progress, meet deadlines,** or **achieve** a **goal**.

3. AN ABILITY TO MAKE MONEY FOR THE COMPANY Explain how your work can **make** or **save money** for the company.

4. AN IMPRESSIVE RÉSUMÉ Highlight the experience and skills that are relevant for each employer, as well as details of your education. Show your résumé to a career counselor or someone with experience in management, and **follow** their **advice**. Their feedback is invaluable.

5. RELEVANT WORK EXPERIENCE Emphasize the **skills** and **knowledge** you **have acquired** in other jobs, and include any relevant **training** you **have had**.

Word sort

B Which nouns in the article go with the words below? Write them in the chart. Then ask a partner which things he or she has done in the last 12 months.

achieve a __goal__	make ________ with a project
acquire ________ or ________	meet a ________
face ________ in school or at work	save or make ________
follow someone's ________	show ________ in a job
have some (job) ________	submit a job ________

Vocabulary notebook

See page 51.

About you

A Have you achieved any goals in the last 12 months?
B Well, one thing I did was pass an accounting exam.

2 Grammar Types of nouns

Figure it out

A Find these three nouns in the article: *candidate, application, research*. Answer the questions below for each noun. Then read the grammar chart.

Is it used with *a/an*?	Is it singular?	Is it plural?

Countable and uncountable nouns

Grammar extra See page 150.

Countable nouns	Uncountable nouns
Countable nouns can be singular. You can use them with *a/an*. *Give **an example** of how you achieved **a goal**.*	Uncountable nouns are only singular. Do not use them with *a/an* or add *-s*. *Explain how your **work** can save **money**.*
Singular countable nouns take a singular verb. Plural countable nouns take a plural verb. ***An impressive résumé is** important.* ***Candidates face** stiff competition.*	Uncountable nouns take a singular verb. ***Feedback** from a counselor **is** invaluable.* ***Research shows** what employers look for.*

Common errors

Don't make these uncountable nouns plural or use them with *a/an* or with plural verbs: *information, equipment, advice, research, knowledge, software, work, homework, training, help, evidence, permission.*

About you

B Complete the questions with a correct form of the nouns given. Sometimes there is more than one answer. Then ask a partner the questions.

1. Do you have a job (job)? How hard is it to find _________ (work) that pays well?
2. Has anyone given you _________ (advice) on your résumé? Did you use the _________ (information)?
3. Do you need _________ (permission) from your school before you take _________ (job)?
4. What do you need to know about _________ (company) before you submit _________ (application)?
5. Where can _________ (graduate) go to get _________ (help) with career planning?
6. What _________ (skill) do you need to start your own business? Where can you get _________ (training)?

C Circle the correct form of the nouns, and write in the correct form of the verb *be*.

"The **information / informations** in the article _________ interesting, especially now when **work / works** _________ hard to find. Any **help / helps** you can get _________ useful. The point about getting **feedback / feedbacks** on your résumé _________ **a good advice / good advice**. My **research / researches** on employers _________ still at an early stage. I want to work in developing **software / softwares**, and I still need **a training / training**, though my **knowledge / knowledges** _________ good."

3 Viewpoint The best advice

Group work **Discuss the questions. Draw up a five-point plan with the best advice for landing your dream job. Read your classmates' plans. How are they different from yours?**

- Which advice in the article on page 42 is most relevant to you right now?
- What do you personally need to do to make sure you land your dream job?
- What else do candidates need to do to stand out in today's job market?

"Actually, the best advice for me was about the relevant work experience."

In conversation . . .

You can use *actually* to give new information.

4 Speaking naturally Word stress *See page 139.*

Lesson B *Perks and benefits*

1 Grammar in context

A **What are some common perks and benefits that people have at work? Share ideas.**

B CD 2.05 **Read the survey. Which perks or benefits are common? Which had you not heard of?**

In a recent poll, 65% of companies believe perks help attract employees. Here are some desirable benefits and perks that are offered by a number of major employers. How do you rate them?

RATE THE PERKS

1 = not at all desirable
5 = extremely desirable

I'd like to work for a company that . . .	1	2	3	4	5
offers free transportation to work.					
gives subsidized child care.					
has good health insurance.					
lets you make personal calls from work.					
has a quiet room for employees to take a nap after lunch.					
lets you take the kids to work if you need to.					
offers free exercise classes after work.					
provides an on-site doctor.					
has a salon that gives discounted haircuts.					
lets you listen to music while you work.					
offers regular training or reimburses tuition fees.					
lets you bring your pet to the office.					

What other perks would you like to have?

- ______________________
- ______________________
- ______________________

About you

C Pair work **Add three more perks or benefits that you would like to have. Then rate all the perks on a scale of 1–5.**

A I think free transportation is a great benefit. You could save a lot with that, so I gave that a 5.
B I agree. Monthly subway passes are so expensive. I gave it a 4.

2 Grammar Generalizing and specifying

Figure it out

A Which sentences below contain errors? Use the survey to help you correct them. Then read the grammar chart.

1. Some employers offer the free exercise classes.
2. Others give you dental insurance.
3. Some let you take the kids to office.
4. Some companies have doctor.

Articles

Grammar extra
See page 151.

Generalizing	Specifying
Use *a/an* with a singular countable noun to make a generalization, or when you don't mean a specific person or thing. *I want to work for* ***a company*** *that has* ***a salon****.*	Use *the* when the idea is known to the reader or listener, or when it is clear which specific person or thing you mean. *I'd like to take* ***the kids*** *to* ***the office****.*
Do not use *the* to make generalizations with a plural countable noun or an uncountable noun. ***Classes*** *after work are a great idea.* *I like to listen to* ***music*** *at work.*	Use *the* when you are specific about which thing you mean. ***The classes that I take*** *are very expensive.* *My colleagues don't like* ***the music I listen to****.*

B Circle *a/an, the,* or – (no article) in the conversations. Then practice with a partner.

1. *A* Would you like to work for **a** / **the** / – company that offers **a** / **the** / – benefits like **a** / **the** / – free food?
   B Well, **a** / **the** / – perks are nice, but I think things like **a** / **the** / – paid overtime are better. Actually, **a** / **the** / – company that I work for has **a** / **the** / – good cafeteria. But I just have **a** / **the** / – sandwich at lunch, so free food isn't really worth much to me.
2. *A* If your company had **an** / **the** / – on-site gym, would you use it?
   B Maybe. But I'd prefer **a** / **the** / – pool. Then I could take **a** / **the** / – kids.
3. *A* Do you think perks like **a** / **the** / – free massages are worth having?
   B Oh, yeah. I'd love **a** / – job that has stuff like that. My friend's company has **an** / **the** / – exercise class during **a** / **the** lunch break every day. She loves it.

About you

C Pair work **Take turns asking and answering the questions above. Give your own answers.**

3 Listening and speaking The best perks

A CD 2.06 **Listen to the perks or benefits that five people discuss. Number them 1–5. Then listen again. Complete the specific examples of each perk in the chart.**

____	paid time off	You can get paid leave to work ____________ or ____________.
____	tuition fees	You can get ____________ or extra ____________.
____	flexible work time	You can ____________ early or ____________.
____	a pleasant atmosphere	You work with ____________ people and get ____________.
____	a health club	You get free ____________, and there's ____________.

About you

B Pair work **Which perks are worth giving up a higher salary for? Why? Agree on the top five ideas. Then present your ideas to another pair.**

A I think free meals are worth giving up a higher salary for. Food is expensive.
B Yeah, I agree. And anyway, I hate cooking when I get home in the evening.

Lesson C *Obviously, . . .*

1 Conversation strategy Showing your attitude

A Replace the words in bold with your own ideas. How many ideas can you think of?

1. One factor to consider before taking a job is **the salary**.
2. **Being stuck in an office all day** is definitely not "me."
3. There's a shortage of **nurses**, so that would be a good choice of career.

B CD 2.07 **Listen. What is Tori's job situation right now?**

Jake How are the interviews going? Any luck yet?

Tori Yeah, as a matter of fact, I just had an offer from a biotech company . . . but I'm having second thoughts about it.

Jake And why's that?

Tori Well, it's a fabulous opportunity with a great salary and everything, but you know, I don't know if it's really "me" – being stuck in a lab all day. I'm not sure it would be rewarding enough.

Jake So you're not tempted by the money, then?

Tori Not really. I mean, money *is* a factor, obviously. But seriously, it's not *that* important. As a matter of fact, I've been considering teaching. I just want to do something that involves people more. But I don't know if they need teachers, really.

Jake Well, interestingly enough, I just read an article that said there's a real shortage of science teachers – so, in fact, teaching might be a good choice for you.

C **Notice** how Jake and Tori show their attitude toward what they say by using *-ly* adverbs like these. Find examples in the conversation.

seriously	*(un)fortunately*
obviously / clearly	*interestingly enough*
luckily	*(not) surprisingly*

In conversation . . .

Interestingly, *strangely*, and *oddly* are often used with *enough*.
Importantly is usually used in the expressions *More importantly* . . . or *Most importantly* . . .

About you

D Add *-ly* adverbs to the sentences using the ideas given. Add *enough* where appropriate. Then discuss the sentences with a partner. Which are true in your situation?

1. ________ (fortunate), I made my own career choices. My parents never forced me into a career I didn't want. ________ (lucky), I've never had second thoughts, either.
2. One of my friends is stuck in a job he really hates, ________ (unfortunate). But ________ (strange), he's not making any effort to leave.
3. ________ (odd), I've never really been tempted by money. I mean, ________ (obvious) a good salary is nice to have. But ________ (more important), you want a job that's really "you."
4. It takes years to train to be a doctor, ________ (not surprising). I mean, doctors make a lot of money, but ________ (serious), I don't want to be in school that long.
5. ________ (interesting), one of my friends has just had a job offer. ________ (unfortunate), they didn't offer him any benefits.

2 Strategy plus *As a matter of fact*

CD 2.08 You can use ***As a matter of fact*** or ***In fact*** to give new information that you want to emphasize.

You can also correct what someone assumes or expects.

There's a real shortage of science teachers – so ***in fact****, teaching might be a good choice.*

A CD 2.09 **Match each question with two answers. Write the letters a–f. Then listen and check.**

1. Have you decided what your next career move will be? ____ ____
2. Do you know anyone who has had second thoughts about their job or career? ____ ____
3. Do you think some people still expect to stay in the same job all their lives? ____ ____

a. I don't think so. In fact, most people's careers change and develop over time.
b. Not really. As a matter of fact, most of my friends love their work.
c. Yeah, I have, as a matter of fact. I'm planning on going into engineering.
d. No. As a matter of fact, nowadays most people are forced to change jobs every few years.
e. Actually, yeah. One of my friends hates his job. In fact, he's looking for something else, so . . .
f. No, I haven't. In fact, I probably should start thinking about that.

About you

B Pair work **Discuss the questions in Exercise A. Use *In fact* and *As a matter of fact* in your answers.**

3 Strategies Changing careers

A CD 2.10 **Circle the best expressions to complete the conversation. Then listen and check your answers. Practice in groups of three.**

Branka I wonder why people change careers.
Josh Well, **obviously, / oddly enough,** a higher salary is one reason.
Pam Yeah. **Unfortunately, / Luckily,** I have a pretty good salary, so . . .
Josh What if your job isn't very rewarding? **In fact, / Fortunately,** that happened to a friend of mine, and he quit his job. **Fortunately, / Seriously,** it worked out for him.
Pam And **luckily, / not surprisingly,** people just get bored.
Branka That's true. **Clearly, / Amazingly,** you don't want to be stuck in a job that's not challenging.
Josh And **in fact, / oddly enough,** it's a good way to get other experience.
Pam **Interestingly enough, / Clearly,** I read an article that said there'll be no more "jobs for life."
Josh I saw that, too, **as a matter of fact / seriously**. We'll all be changing jobs and **more importantly, / strangely enough,** going back to school!

About you

B Pair work **Agree on six good reasons to change careers. What are good reasons not to change careers? Make a list of your ideas.**

"Well, one reason would be because you're bored with the career you have. Obviously, if your job's not rewarding enough, you'll get tired of it and . . ."

Reasons to change careers . . .
1. It's not rewarding enough . . .
Reasons not to change careers . . .

Lesson D *Ace that interview!*

1 Reading

A **Prepare Which of these are good questions for a candidate to ask at a job interview? Which are not? Why?**

a. How does the position fit into the company's structure?
b. What opportunities are there to get training?
c. What projects are you currently working on?
d. Can I work from home?
e. How is performance reviewed?
f. How much vacation will I get?

B **Read for main ideas Read the article. Where do the questions in Exercise A fit in the article? Write the questions.**

CAREER Help

What questions should I ask at a job interview?

1 Congratulations! After submitting dozens of applications, you've finally landed an interview. You've done your research on the company, printed out extra copies of your résumé, and even rehearsed answers to questions like, "What is your greatest weakness?" But have you prepared for the most difficult interview question of all: "Do you have any questions for us?"

2 "A candidate can't afford to trip up on this question," says Erica Lee, a career advisor in Los Angeles. "Employers need evidence that you're interested in the position." To avoid this fate, follow Lee's advice and impress your future boss by asking questions like these:

3 [1.] ____________________
"Listen carefully to the answer," advises Lee. "Then show how you can help them achieve their goals." Try to sell yourself as a solution to a manager's problems. "Managers spend most of their time worrying," says Lee. "Clearly, an employee who takes that stress away is like gold to them."

4 [2.] ____________________
Employers want people who care about the company as a whole, not just about their own paycheck. Lee says this question also helps you see if the job has long-term potential. "If they make the job sound unimportant, do you really want to be working there five years from now?"

5 [3.] ____________________
This shows your desire to acquire skills and knowledge that will benefit the company. In addition, says Lee, "it shows you're interested in working your way up the organization. You want a promotion – who doesn't? – but you are willing to work for it."

6 [4.] ____________________
This question demonstrates that you appreciate the importance of being accountable, meeting deadlines and targets. It also shows that you understand the value of constructive criticism and guidance.

7 Lee also warns her clients *not* to ask questions like these.

8 [5.] ____________________
If you ask this, employers will worry that you're not fully committed to the job. "Focus on getting offered the job first," says Lee. "Then you can discuss annual leave, benefits, and, of course, compensation."

9 [6.] ____________________
It's never a good idea to show an interest in this at the interview. "The managers I know all prefer staff to work in the office first to make an assessment of their work and training needs," says Lee. "Again, just try to get the job first." Similarly, avoid questions like, "Do I have to work overtime?" or "Can I listen to music at work?"

10 Remember an interview is a two-way process. You need to find out if the job is right for you, so don't be afraid to ask questions. Just make sure they're the right ones.

Reading tip

Writers use *this* (instead of *it* or *that*) when they focus on something important. (See paragraphs 5 and 8.)

C Paraphrase **Read the sentences below. Underline the sentences in the article that they paraphrase.**

1. You need to prepare not just to answer questions but to *ask* questions, too.
2. Interviewees shouldn't make a mistake when answering this question.
3. Workers who are able to deal with difficult problems are extremely valuable.
4. It demonstrates you are willing to learn new skills to make the company more successful.
5. Asking this question shows you see the benefit of getting useful feedback.
6. Make sure you don't give the impression that you won't be dedicated to your work.

About you

D React **Which parts of the article did you find most useful? Which questions have you asked at an interview? What other questions should you ask?**

2 Focus on vocabulary Word families

About you

Complete the sentences with the noun form of the words given. Use the article to help you. Then work with a partner. Give examples from your own experience.

Give an example of . . .

1. how you usually find a _________ to a difficult problem. (solve)
2. the _________ of preparing for an interview. (important)
3. a skill you have that employers put a high _________ on. (value)
4. a time someone gave you constructive _________. (criticize)
5. a time you offered someone _________ on something important. (guide)
6. a good way to make an _________ of a future employer. (assess)
7. a skill that most employers have a _________ for. (need)

"If I need to find a solution to a difficult problem, I usually think of all the possible options and . . ."

3 Listening and speaking Interview rules . . .

A Pair work **Read the advice a–e about how to answer interview questions. Why are these good rules to follow? What other rules can you think of?**

Candidate	Advice: when you answer interview questions, . . .
1. Elizabeth	a. give actual examples of relevant experience to support your answers.
2. Marcus	b. be clear and concise, but don't just say yes or no.
3. Esma	c. never criticize a professor or previous boss.
4. Carlos	d. don't try to be funny.
5. Hugo	e. be prepared beforehand so you know what to expect.

B CD 2.11 **Listen to extracts from five interviews. Match each person in Exercise A with the rule he or she breaks. Draw lines.**

About you

C CD 2.12 **Think of a job you might want to interview for. Listen to the interview questions again, and prepare your own answers. Then compare answers with a partner.**

"For question 1 I wrote, I've applied for this position as a receptionist because I'd like to work in a job that gives me opportunities to use my English."

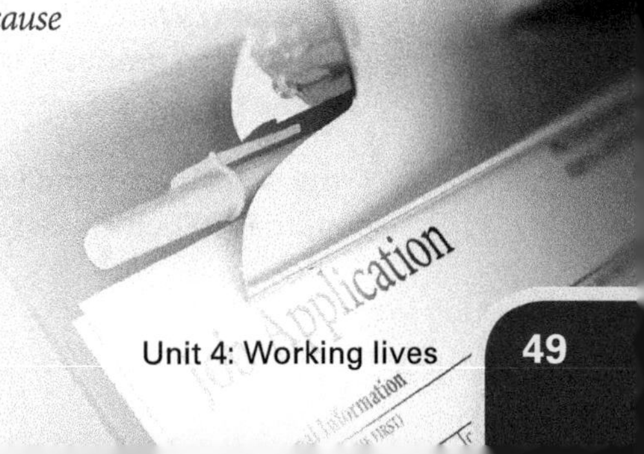

Writing *My responsibilities included . . .*

In this lesson, you . . .
- use paragraphs for different topics.
- use nouns in formal writing.
- avoid errors with uncountable nouns.

Task Write a personal statement.
Give personal information in support of an application.

A **Look at a model** **Read the excerpts from a personal statement on an application for a graduate program. Which topic does each paragraph address? Write the letters a–e.**

a. Introduction b. Leisure time c. Studies d. Summary e. Work experience

1. ☐ My interest in business began in high school. I was team leader of the investment club. My responsibilities included organizing the meetings and writing reports. (. . .)
2. ☐ In college my major was financial management, which is critical to the success of any company. (. . .)
3. ☐ Last year I completed an internship in the management office of a hotel, which gave me some invaluable experience in meeting deadlines and achieving goals. The decision to do this internship was based on my wish to pursue a career in the hospitality industry. (. . .)
4. ☐ In my free time, I volunteer at a senior center. This experience has taught me the importance of patience and understanding. (. . .)
5. ☐ I am now ready to take on a further challenge by studying for a master's degree in business administration. (. . .)

B **Focus on language** **How does the writer express the ideas below? Underline the sentences in the personal statement in Exercise A. Then read the grammar chart.**

I was interested in business. I was responsible for writing reports. I decided to do this internship.

Using nouns in formal writing

Use nouns to make your writing more formal and varied. Don't start every sentence with *I* + verb.

I was interested in business in high school. → ***My interest*** *in business began in high school.*

I was responsible for writing reports. → ***My responsibilities*** *included writing reports.*

I decided to do this internship. → ***The decision*** *to do this internship was based on . . .*

C **Rewrite the sentences, using noun forms of the words in bold.**

1. I was **responsible** for advertising student events and raising money. My responsibilities included . . .
2. I have grown more **interested** in the media over the last three years.
3. I **worked** in a software company, and it helped me improve my time-management skills.
4. I **decided** to go into nursing because I **wish** to pursue a career in caregiving.

D **Brainstorm** **Write ideas for an application to college, to graduate school, or for a job. Use the model in Exercise A to help you.**

E **Write and check** **Write your personal statement. Then check for errors.**

Common errors

Check your use of uncountable nouns.

This gave me ***some*** *invaluable* ***experience****.*
(NOT ~~*an*~~ *invaluable* ~~*experience*~~)

My work ***experience*** *includes an internship at a hotel.*
(NOT ~~*experiences include*~~)

I would like ***a job / a position*** *in hotel management.*
(NOT ~~*a work*~~)

Vocabulary notebook *Meet that deadline!*

Learning tip Collocations

When you learn a new word, write down its collocations – the words that are used with it. For example, write the verbs and adjectives that go with a noun.

have, meet, miss, set a deadline
a tight deadline

A Complete the vocabulary notes with the verbs in the box.

achieve acquire ✔ face follow make make save show submit

1. face competition
2. ________ or ________ money
3. ________ progress
4. ________ interest
5. ________ an application
6. ________ knowledge
7. ________ a goal
8. ________ advice

B Look back at page 42. Write an adjective that can go before each noun. Can you add other adjectives?

1. stiff competition
2. ________ job
3. ________ résumé
4. ________ skills
5. ________ feedback
6. ________ training

C Word builder Add nouns from Exercises A and B to these sets of verbs and adjectives. Sometimes there is more than one answer.

Verbs

1. give, offer, take, ignore, seek advice
2. fill out, complete ________
3. set, achieve, reach ________

Adjectives

1. fierce, intense ________
2. positive, negative ________
3. formal, vocational ________
4. social, technical ________
5. good, practical, helpful ________

Dictionary tip

Dictionaries often tell you if a noun is countable [C], uncountable [U], or both [C/U]. Read the example sentences to find a noun's collocations.

interest (INVOLVEMENT)
noun [C/U]
I lost interest halfway through the book.

On your own

Make a poster for your own career goal. Write a career goal in the center of the poster, and then write all the things you have to do to achieve it. Put the poster on your wall.

Unit 5

Challenges

In Unit 5, you . . .

- talk about world issues and ways to help.
- use conditional sentences to talk about wishes, hopes, and regrets.
- use *what if*, *suppose*, and *imagine* to suggest possible scenarios or ideas.
- use *I suppose* to show you're not 100 percent sure.

Lesson A *Giving away your things*

1 Grammar in context

A **Are there a lot of homeless people in your area? How do people generally react toward the homeless?**

B CD 2.13 **Read the article. What did Hannah Salwen's family do and why?**

THE POWER OF *half*

What would you do if you saw a homeless person begging in the street? Walk on by? Give a few spare coins? Not the Salwen family . . . they gave much more than that. Read their story and ask yourself, *"What would I have done?"*

Kevin Salwen was driving his 14-year-old daughter, Hannah, back from a sleepover. Hannah had often seen homeless people begging for food at the stoplight near their home. But on this particular day, while they were waiting for the light, Hannah noticed an expensive car in front of them and a homeless man standing on the side of the road.

"If that guy didn't have such a nice car, the man over here could have a meal," Hannah said. The scene clearly made a deep impression on Hannah, and she continued to discuss it with her parents and brother for some time. She wanted her family to make a difference in the world – even if it was a small difference.

"How much are you willing to give up?" her mom asked. "This house?" Eventually, that's exactly what the family did. They sold their $2 million dream home and donated half the proceeds to the Hunger Project's work in Africa.

The Salwen family in front of the house they sold

If Hannah hadn't seen the homeless man alongside the car that day, maybe the Salwens would still be in their dream home. But would they be as happy? In their new, smaller house, they found they were spending more time together and became closer as a family. They admit they might not have become so close if they had stayed in their old home.

If you want to learn more about the Salwens' remarkable story, visit their website.

C Pair work **Close your book. Then retell the story with a partner. How much detail can you remember?**

2 Grammar Imagining situations

Figure it out

A Circle the correct verb forms to complete the sentences below. Use the article to help you. Then read the grammar chart.

1. What would you do if you **see** / **saw** a homeless person?
2. The family might not **have become** / **become** so close if they hadn't moved to a smaller house.
3. If Hannah **didn't see** / **hadn't seen** the man and the car, the family might still live in the big house.

Conditional statements and questions

Grammar extra
See page 152.

You can use *if* clauses to talk about hypothetical events in the present or past. Notice the commas.

Present *If* + past form; modal + verb	*What **would** you **do** if you **saw** a homeless person on the street?* *If he **looked** hungry, **I'd** probably **give** him some money.*
Past *If* + past perfect form; modal + *have* + past participle	*If you**'d been** in the car with Hannah, what **would** you **have done**?* *I **might not have thought** about it if she **hadn't mentioned** it.*
Mixed present and past	*If they still **lived** in their big house, **would** they **have raised** any money?* *Maybe. But they **might not be** so close now if they **had stayed** there.*

About you

B Complete the conversations with a correct form of the verbs given. Sometimes there is more than one correct answer. Then ask the questions and give your own answers.

1. *A* Would the Salwens have had (have) the idea to sell their home, do you think, if Hannah ________ (not see) the expensive car that day?
   B Maybe not. If the car ________ (not stop) in front of them, she ________ (might not decide) to do something. But maybe she ________ (do) something later.
2. *A* If you ________ (be) in the car with Hannah that day, how ________ you ________ (react)?
   B You mean, if I ________ (see) the homeless man, too? I ________ (not do) anything.
3. *A* If you ________ (be) Hannah, how would you have ________ (feel) when the house was sold?
   B I ________ (be) really upset if I ________ (have to) move. But I guess I ________ (agree) to it.
4. *A* What ________ you ________ (do) if someone ________ (ask) you for money on the street?
   B It depends. Maybe I'd give them a few coins – if I ________ (have) change.

3 Listening and speaking What would you give away?

A CD 2.14 **Listen to three people talk about ways to help others. Number the summaries of what they say 1–3. Then listen again and complete the sentences for each person.**

If I wanted to help, I'd . . .	I'd be able to do it if I . . .	I'd give to . . .
☐ use the car less.		
☐ donate my time.		
☐ watch my spending on groceries.		

About you

B Class activity **Make a chart like the one above, and ask your classmates questions. Complete the chart with your classmates' ideas.**

"So, what would you do if you wanted to do something for charity?"

Lesson B *A better future?*

1 Vocabulary in context

A CD 2.15 **What are some of the biggest problems that the world faces today? Make a list. Then listen to four people. Which of your ideas are mentioned?**

WE ASKED PEOPLE, **"WHAT'S THE BIGGEST CHALLENGE FACING THE WORLD TODAY?"**

Here are some of their views and hopes for the future.

"Well, I wish we could **eradicate poverty**. The gap between the rich and the poor keeps getting bigger. There's something like two billion people who live below the poverty line. I just wish we **distributed wealth** more fairly."

"I guess I'd choose **protecting** the **environment**. And **pollution** is, I think, the biggest problem. I just wish everywhere hadn't gotten so **polluted**. **Environmental protection** is critical if we're going to survive. I also wish we **invested** more in "green" projects. I hope that makes sense."

"The biggest challenge? The **eradication** of **hunger**. I really wish someone would find a solution. You see all these **poor, starving** people – 16,000 kids die every day from **starvation**. No one should be **hungry** in this day and age. The problem is mostly one of food **distribution**. There are enough **wealthy** countries to solve it. I just wish I knew what to do about it."

"Um, there are so many **unemployed** people, especially with the economy the way it is right now. I wish the government would do something to reduce **unemployment** and **create** new jobs. I hope they put more **investment** in job **creation**."

About you

B Circle the correct form of the words to complete the sentences. Then discuss the sentences with a partner. Do any reflect your views?

1. **Unemployed / Unemployment** is not a big problem. There's plenty of **invest / investment** in jobs.
2. There's no solution to the problem of **poor / poverty**. Its **eradicate / eradication** is impossible.
3. There's definitely a problem with the distribution of **wealth / wealthy**.
4. I know people are **starving / starvation**, but **hungry / hunger** isn't the biggest issue.
5. My priority would be environmental **protect / protection** – sorting out **polluted / pollution**.
6. There should be more job **create / creation** programs for young people.

Word sort

C Write the words in bold in the article in a chart like this. Add any other words you know. Then, in pairs, use each noun in a sentence about world problems.

Noun	Verb	Adjective
poverty	—	poor

Vocabulary notebook

See page 61.

2 **Grammar** Talking about wishes, hopes, and regrets

Figure it out

A Are the sentences below true (T) or false (F)? Write T or F. Underline the sentences in the interviews that tell you. Then read the grammar chart.

1. Aya thinks that wealth is distributed fairly. ____
2. Luis feels bad that the world has become polluted. ____
3. Pin says someone has found a solution to hunger. ____
4. Tom wants someone to invest in new jobs. ____

wish and *hope*

Grammar extra
See page 153.

Use *wish* + past form to imagine a different situation in the present.	*Aya wishes we* ***could*** *eradicate poverty. She wishes the gap between rich and poor* ***was / were*** *smaller.*
Use *wish* + past perfect to imagine the past.	*Luis wishes everywhere* ***hadn't gotten*** *so polluted.*
Use *wish* + *would* + verb for things you want other people to do or for things you can't control.	*Pin wishes someone* ***would solve*** *the hunger problem.* *Tom wishes the government* ***would do*** *something.*
Use *hope* to talk about things that you want to be true about the future, present, or past.	*Tom hopes they* ***(will) create*** *more new jobs.* *I hope that* ***makes*** *sense / I* ***didn't say*** *anything silly.*

In conversation . . .

I wish I were . . . and *I wish it were . . .* are considered correct in writing. However, people often say *I wish I was . . .* and *I wish it was . . .*

About you

B Rewrite the sentences starting with the words given. Sometimes there is more than one answer. Then discuss the sentences with a partner. Do any of them represent your views?

1. Big industries shouldn't pollute the rivers. *I wish . . .*
   I wish big industries wouldn't / didn't pollute the rivers.
2. Someone needs to do something to help the homeless. *I hope . . .*
3. The government should have invested in public transportation years ago. *I wish . . .*
4. It's difficult to find a solution to problems like starvation and hunger. *I wish . . .*
5. Governments need to do more to protect wildlife, but they probably won't. *I wish . . .*
6. I don't know how to eradicate poverty in our cities. *I wish . . .*
7. We shouldn't have ignored all the environmental problems in our country. *I wish . . .*
8. I didn't want to upset you when we were discussing the distribution of wealth. *I hope . . .*

3 **Viewpoint** Good solutions

A Pair work **How can we make the world a better place? Complete the sentences.**

I wish we could . . .
I wish we hadn't . . .
I hope our government will . . .
I hope people won't . . .
I wish more people would . . .

B Group work **Discuss your sentences. Decide on the three most pressing problems, and figure out some possible solutions. Present your ideas to the class.**

A *I wish we could do something like eradicate all the diseases in the world.*
B *Oh, definitely. Maybe if wealthy countries made cheaper vaccines, it would help.*

In conversation . . .

You can use *Absolutely* or *Definitely* to agree strongly with someone.

4 **Speaking naturally** Shifting word stress *See page 140.*

Lesson C *What if . . . ?*

1 Conversation strategy Imagining possible scenarios

A Would you consider doing any of these things for charity? Why? Why not?

plant a tree   adopt a polar bear   sponsor a child

B CD 2.18 Listen. What does Lucia think about buying gifts? What does Jim think?

Lucia I wish I knew what to get my nephew for his birthday. I should have thought about it earlier, and I wouldn't be in this last-minute panic now.

Jim I suppose there's no point in getting him just another toy.

Lucia Yeah. You know, the average kid here has 150 toys, which is unbelievable. It's just ridiculous . . .

Jim I suppose it is.

Lucia . . . especially when there's so much poverty in the world. I mean, suppose everybody gave to charity instead of buying useless gifts.

Jim But just imagine you were five years old and you got this card from your aunt that said she planted a tree for you somewhere. I mean, how disappointed would *you* feel?

Lucia I suppose. Well, what if I adopted a polar bear for him?

C **Notice** how Lucia and Jim use *what if . . . ?* and the imperatives *suppose* and *imagine* to suggest possible scenarios or ideas. Find the examples in the conversation.

I mean, suppose everybody gave to charity . . .

In conversation . . .

What if . . . ? is the most common of these expressions. It is mostly used in follow-up questions. It doesn't usually start a conversation.

About you

D Complete the conversations with *suppose, what if,* or *imagine.* There may be more than one answer. Then practice with a partner. Practice again, giving your own answers.

1. *A* _________ you wanted to buy an unusual gift for a kid. What would you get? A microscope?
   B Maybe, but _________ you didn't really know the kid? It would be hard to choose, huh?
2. *A* _________ a friend planted a tree for your birthday. How would you feel?
   B Good question. I'm not sure. Yeah, . . . or _________ they adopted an animal or something?
3. *A* _________ you had to buy a last-minute gift for a friend. What would you do?
   B Oh, I'd probably just get a gift card. Something easy.
4. *A* _________ a friend wanted to give to a charity in your name. Which one would you choose?
   B Oh, um, . . . maybe a children's hospital or something. But _________ I really wanted a gift?

2 Strategy plus *I suppose*

CD 2.19 You can use ***I suppose*** when you're not 100 percent sure or don't want to sound 100 percent sure.

I suppose can also be a response, to show the other person is right or has a good point.

A *It's just ridiculous.*
B ***I suppose (it is).***

In conversation . . .

I suppose is more common in a full sentence than as a response.

I suppose (that) . . .   *I suppose.*

A CD 2.20 **Match each question with two answers. Write the letters a–f. Then listen and check. Practice with a partner.**

1. Don't you think it's hard shopping for gifts? _____ _____
2. Do you always buy birthday cards for people? _____ _____
3. Do you ever "re-gift" unwanted presents? You know, pass them on to other people? _____ _____

a. I suppose I do. But I'll often just send an e-mail if it's last minute.
b. No, never. I suppose I'd worry that someone would find out!
c. Usually. I do it because I like to get lots on my own birthday, I suppose.
d. Actually, I enjoy it. Though I suppose it's not easy if you don't know what people want.
e. Sometimes. I suppose it's better than keeping something you don't want.
f. I suppose. Usually, I buy gift cards so people can choose what they want.

About you

B Pair work **Take turns asking the questions above. Give your own answers using *I suppose*.**

3 Strategies Make the world a fairer place.

About you

A Group work **Discuss the ideas for making the world a fairer place. How many other ideas can you add? Which could you do easily?**

- Buy fair trade products from companies that pay farmers or workers a fair price.
- Join a campaign for clean drinking water for everyone.
- Participate in a sponsored walk, run, or other event to raise money for a charity.
- Sign a petition to support women's rights.
- Volunteer to help disadvantaged children learn to read.

A *Suppose we only bought fair trade coffee. Then farmers would get a fair price.*
B *That's true. I suppose we could do that for other foods, too.*

B Pair work **Agree on one idea that you would like the class to adopt. Prepare a presentation to "sell" your idea to the class. Vote on the best idea.**

Lesson D *Mercy Ships*

1 Reading

A Prepare **Look at the photos and the title. Can you guess what the article is about?**

B Read for main ideas **Read the exclusive interview. What does the Mercy Ships organization do? How is Dr. Cheng involved?**

ON THE Mercy Ships

An interview with Dr. Leo Cheng

Q: Can you tell us what the Mercy Ships are and what kind of work they do?

Dr. Cheng: Mercy Ships run a hospital ship that brings world-class surgical and medical services to people in countries where there is a need. The organization Mercy Ships was started by Don and Deyon Stephens. Don and Deyon were caught in the Caribbean during a huge tropical storm, which caused a lot of devastation. There was a girl sitting beside them, and she was shaking – very cold – and praying for a ship to come and help the injured and sick, and to bring supplies to rebuild the hospitals and schools and so on. That gave them their vision, and since 1978, Mercy Ships has been doing just that – bringing hope and healing and rebuilding lives. If Don and Deyon hadn't been caught in that storm, they might not have had the idea for the Mercy Ships.

Q: So, what do you do on the Mercy Ships? Can you tell us about your work?

Dr. Cheng: I trained as a dentist, then a doctor, and then a general surgeon. I specialize in the head and neck areas, and I remove benign lumps or tumors. Here in the UK, it takes half an hour to treat a patient, but the problem in many developing countries is that a small lump doesn't get treated, so it grows into something enormous. That's something that we don't see here.

Q: If you hadn't worked on the Mercy Ships, do you think you'd be a different person today?

Dr. Cheng: Definitely. I would be a very different person. When I first went to work for Mercy Ships, my life changed. Everybody is there to offer service to others. We do not get a salary. We do not have a pension. We have to pay our own expenses to travel out there, which is not cheap.

Q: How does your work change people's lives? Can you give me an example?

Dr. Cheng: Well, let me tell you about a grandmother who came to the ship, and then you'll understand how the surgery changed her life. This woman had a large growth on her neck. She realized that her grandchildren were no longer sitting on her lap, and she was devastated and spent all her time alone. Her only wish was that her grandchildren would sit on her lap again. The night before surgery, she said, "I'm so looking forward to hugging my grandchildren and to putting them on my knee again." And obviously, to her, that was her pride and joy. The surgery brought joy back into her life. There are a lot of stories like that.

Mercy Ships is an international charity that provides free medical care and humanitarian aid. Over the last 30 years, it has worked in more than 70 countries, performed over 56,000 surgeries, and completed more than 1,000 community-development projects focusing on water, sanitation, and agriculture and impacting about 2.9 million people.

C Read for detail **Complete the sentences about the article. Then compare with a partner.**

1. If Don and Deyon Stephens hadn't been in the Caribbean, ________________ .
2. If Dr. Cheng hadn't worked with Mercy Ships, he thinks ________________ .
3. If the grandmother hadn't had surgery, ________________ .
4. If Mercy Ships didn't exist, millions of people ________________ .

2 Focus on vocabulary Word building

A **Look for these words in the article. Find . . .**

1. two words with the root form *devastate*: __________ , __________
2. two words with the same meaning as *tumor*: __________ , __________
3. three words that mean the same as *big*: __________ , __________ , __________
4. a word that means the opposite of *harmful* or *malignant*: __________
5. three different professions: __________ , __________ , __________
6. three words that refer to people who need treatment: __________ , __________ , __________

B Pair work **Take turns using the words in Exercise A to describe the work of Mercy Ships.**

"Don and Deyon Stephens got their vision for Mercy Ships when they saw all the devastation in the Caribbean and . . ."

3 Listening and speaking Inspiring people

A CD 2.21 **Listen to another interview with Dr. Cheng. Check (✔) the things he talks about.**

- ☐ How to help Mercy Ships
- ☐ The jobs that are available with Mercy Ships
- ☐ How he spends his free time on the ships
- ☐ What he does during a typical surgery
- ☐ An ordinary woman who wanted to help
- ☐ What Dr. Cheng plans to do in retirement

B CD 2.22 **Listen again. Are the sentences true (T) or false (F)? Write T or F. Compare answers with a partner. Correct the false information.**

1. The only people who work on the ships are skilled doctors and nurses. _____
2. Dr. Cheng's daughter has also worked on the ships as a surgeon. _____
3. Dr. Cheng gives presentations and talks about his work with Mercy Ships. _____
4. One woman who was inspired by Dr. Cheng donated all her income. _____
5. Mercy Ships can only accept people who want to work long-term. _____

About you

C Group work **Discuss the questions.**

- If you had the opportunity to help Mercy Ships, what would you do? What skills could you offer?
- How do you think people benefit from working with the organization?
- What other programs do you know about that help people around the world?

"Well, I wish I could do something to help. If I hadn't just started a job, I'd volunteer to help in the kitchens or something."

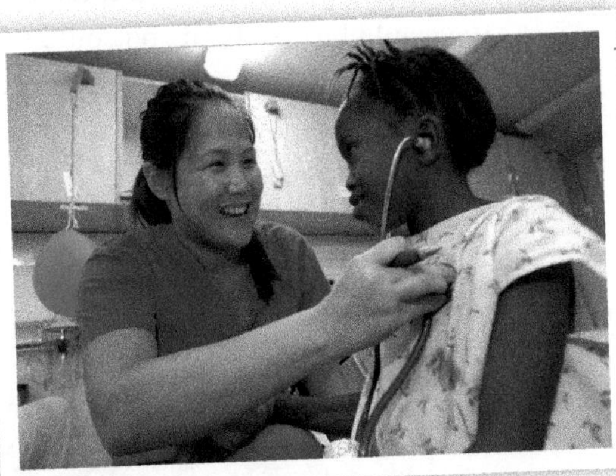

Writing *Volunteering*

In this lesson, you . . .

- make a polite inquiry.
- use *it* as a subject and an object.
- avoid errors with verb subjects.

Task **Write an inquiry.**

Write an email inquiry to a volunteer program.

A Look at a model **Read the email. Underline the sentences where Mary asks for information.**

Contact Form Get Involved

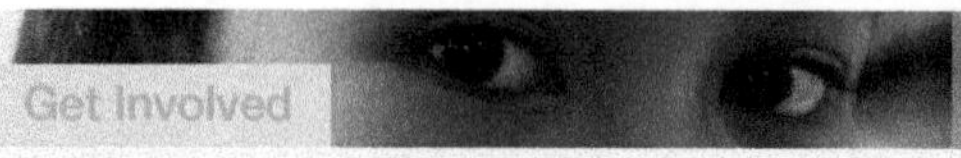

volunteer

Your Message:

Dear Sir or Madam:

I would like to volunteer with your program as an English-teaching assistant in July. I have read the information on your website and have a number of queries.

Your website says that the programs run from Saturday to Saturday. I would find it difficult to arrive on Saturday. Would it be a problem if I joined the program on Sunday? Also, I would appreciate it if you could send me more details about the accommodations.

In addition, it would be useful if I could talk to someone who has volunteered with you before. Is there anyone I can contact in my area?

Thank you for your assistance. I look forward to hearing from you.

Sincerely,

Mary L. Griffin

SUBMIT

B Focus on language **Read the grammar chart. Then read sentences from the organization's reply below. Add *it* to the sentences where necessary.**

Dummy *it* in writing

It can be a subject.	***It*** *would be* ***useful*** *if I could talk to someone in my area.* *Would* ***it*** *be* ***a problem*** *if I joined the program on Sunday?*
Use *it* as an object after these verbs.	*I would* ***appreciate it*** *if you could send details.* *I would* ***find it*** *difficult to arrive on Saturday.*

In conversation . . .

People often use *love* in this way.

I would ***love it*** *if you could come over on Saturday.*

1. We would prefer if you could arrive on Saturday, because we do the training that evening.
2. We would appreciate if you could confirm your arrival time as soon as possible.
3. We would be grateful if you could send your payment for the accommodations.
4. You will find useful to talk to someone about volunteering.
5. There are volunteers in your town, so is not a problem to put you in touch with someone.

Common errors

Avoid using a form of *be* to start a statement.

It *would be useful to talk to someone.* (NOT ~~*Would be useful . . .*~~)

C Write and check **Write an inquiry with questions to a program below. Then check for errors.**

Help build a home for a family. Work in a wildlife sanctuary. Help serve meals to the needy.

Vocabulary notebook *Wealthy = rich*

Learning tip **Synonyms and paraphrases**

To help you remember a new word, write down its synonyms – words with a similar meaning. If there isn't a synonym, write a paraphrase – an expression with a similar meaning.

wealthy = rich
to eradicate = to get rid of
poverty = being poor

A **Match the words on the left with the synonyms and paraphrases on the right. Draw lines.**

1. pollution
2. distribution
3. protection
4. hunger
5. unemployed
6. to invest

a. giving out
b. out of work
c. being very hungry / having too little food
d. to spend or put money into
e. caring for; keeping safe
f. damage to the environment, e.g., to water or air

B **Now write synonyms or paraphrases for these words.**

1. to protect ____________________
2. starving ____________________
3. to pollute ____________________
4. to distribute ____________________
5. to create ____________________

C **Word builder** **Find the meanings of these words. Write synonyms or paraphrases to help you learn them.**

1. abolish ____________________
2. conservation ____________________
3. destruction ____________________
4. population ____________________
5. resource ____________________

What do we want to *eradicate?*

These are the things people write most about eradicating: *poverty, disease* (*polio, malaria*), *drugs, racism, corruption, illiteracy,* and *homelessness.*

On your own

Make a list of the news stories you see or hear this week.

I saw / heard . . .
a report on river pollution.
a story about an unemployed father.

Unit 6

Into the future

In Unit 6, you . . .

- talk about money, technology, and future developments.
- describe future events.
- use modal verbs to express different meanings.
- soften your opinions with *would*.
- use *so* in responses like *I think so* to avoid repeating words.

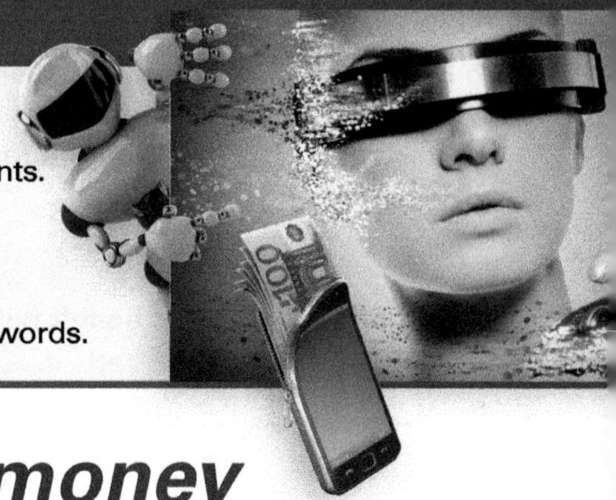

Lesson A *The future of money*

1 Grammar in context

A How many different ways are there to pay for things? Which ways do you prefer?

"Well, you can use a credit or debit card. I tend to use my credit card because . . ."

B CD 2.23 **Listen to four students' comments from a class discussion. What different ways of paying for things do the students mention?**

Professor: So, imagine the headline 20 years from now: *Only one day left to turn in your old coins and bills.* Is this really going to happen? And if it does, what will it be like, do you think, to have a cashless society?

Amanda: Well, I mean, most people don't carry much cash now – I mostly use my debit card, and for bigger things, I use a credit card. So I think people are going to be using a lot less cash in the future. And in 20 years, we'll probably be doing all our shopping online, so there may not be a need for cash then.

Sam: I agree that everyone's going to use credit cards more. But the problem is, if we don't have better security, then there'll be more fraud and identity theft and everything. It's just a thought, but if paper money becomes obsolete, then our grandchildren might be looking at it in museums!

Oliver: But if we only use credit cards, then what are kids going to do? Will they have to carry prepaid debit cards? It just seems unlikely to me. I mean, we might see less cash in the future, but it won't be disappearing anytime soon. Though I have to say, it'll be good to get rid of those small coins.

Judith: I think in the future, every phone will have a chip that carries all our personal information – you know, our bank details and everything. We may not even need credit or debit cards. So you'll just use your cell phone when you buy things. It's already happening in some parts of the world, which is interesting.

C Answer the questions about the comments in Exercise B. Check (✓) the names.

Who thinks that in the future . . .	Amanda	Oliver	Sam	Judith
1. there could be problems with a cashless society?				
2. a cashless society is inevitable?				
3. credit cards are likely to become more popular?				
4. credit cards are likely to disappear?				
5. we're less likely to shop in stores?				

2 Grammar Describing future events

Figure it out

A Complete the summaries of the discussion on page 62 using the same verb forms that the students use. Then read the grammar chart.

1. Amanda thinks it's clear that people ________ (use) a lot less cash in the future.
2. Oliver says cash ________ (not disappear) anytime soon.
3. Sam thinks that his grandchildren ________ (look) at paper money in museums one day.
4. Judith says you ________ just ________ (use) a cell phone when you ________ (buy) things.

Future events with *be going to, will, may, might*

Grammar extra
See page 154.

Use a continuous form after *be going to, will, may,* and *might* for events you expect to be in progress at a future time.

You can use *be going to* when there's evidence now for a future event.	*Everyone**'s going to use** cards more in the future.* *We**'re (not) going to be using** cash 20 years from now.*
You can use *will, may,* or *might* in predictions. *Will* is more certain than *may* or *might.*	*Every cell phone **will** (probably) **have** a chip.* *Cash (probably) **won't be disappearing** soon.* *There **may not be** a need for cash.* *We **might be using** phones.*
Use the present form in *if* or time clauses that refer to the future.	*If we only **use** cards, what are kids going to do?* *You'll use your cell phone when you **buy** things in the future.*

In conversation . . .

The continuous form is mostly used after *will* and *be going to*. *Be going to be + -ing* is not common in writing.

B Circle the correct options to complete the sentences.

1. Coins and bills **disappear / might disappear** in the future.
2. One day we **won't be using / don't use** cash at all. But when cash **will become / becomes** obsolete, I think we **miss / 're going to miss** it.
3. If there**'s / 'll be** no cash in the future, we **won't need / don't need** wallets.
4. We may spend more if we **pay / 'll pay** with credit cards.
5. There probably **aren't / won't be** any real stores because we **shop / 're going to be shopping** online. You**'re not / won't be** able to try on clothes before you**'ll decide / decide** to buy them.
6. I think everyone**'s going to be using / uses** online banking in the future. We **don't have to / won't have to** go into actual banks anymore.

About you

C Pair work **Do you share the opinions in Exercise B? Discuss your ideas.**

"Well, I don't think coins and dollar bills are going to disappear, but they might become less common."

3 Listening Going cashless – the pros and cons!

A CD 2.24 **Listen. Rafael and Luana are talking about the pros and cons of a cashless society. Check (✓) the issues that they discuss.**

☐ 1. convenience _____ ☐ 3. debt _____ ☐ 5. taxes _____
☐ 2. prices _____ ☐ 4. crime _____ ☐ 6. privacy _____

B CD 2.25 **Listen again. What do Rafael and Luana say about each checked issue above? Will it be: a) reduced, b) greater, c) the same? Write the letters a, b, or c above.**

4 Speaking naturally Silent consonants *See page 140.*

Lesson B *Presenting the future*

1 Vocabulary in context

A CD 2.28 **Listen to these extracts from a presentation. What's the general topic of the presentation?**

1 "Hello, everybody. I'm just waiting for the projector – it won't connect. Oh, it must be warming up. It shouldn't take long. There. OK. **Can you all see the screen?** Let's see. I could make it a little bigger. Would somebody turn the lights off, please? Thanks. Um, **there should be a handout going around**, too. All right, **let's get started** . . ."

2 "So, today **I want to look at** the future of clothing. In particular, **I'll be talking about** the impact that technology will have on the clothes we wear. **I'll allow time for questions and comments at the end.** So, **I'd like to begin by** thinking about the question, 'What will our clothes be able to *do* in the future?' For example, we already have jackets that light up in the dark for road safety . . ."

3 "**As you'll see on the slide,** there are lots of other possibilities, too, such as clothes that use body energy to recharge cell phones and computers, and clothes that will be able to detect health problems. So, **let's move on** and **look at** ideas like these in more detail . . ."

4 "So as you can see, technology could have an impact on our lives in interesting ways – not least with self-cleaning fabrics. **Anyway, that's all I have time for**. So, **I'd better stop** there. Um, we should have time for one or two questions. **Does anyone have any questions or comments?**"

5 "If you're interested in reading more, you might want to check out some of the articles that are listed on the handout. **I'll just conclude by saying** thank you for listening. And now **I'll turn it over** to John, who's going to talk about clothes that heat or cool on demand . . ."

B Pair work **Cover the presentation and answer the questions. How much can you remember?**

1. What does the speaker do before she starts her presentation?
2. What topic does she specifically talk about?
3. In what ways does she suggest clothing might be different in the future?
4. Why does the speaker have to end her presentation?

Word sort

C **Find expressions that the speaker uses in her presentation to do these things. Complete the chart. Compare with a partner.**

Start the presentation	
Introduce the topic	
Check that everyone can see or hear	Can you all see the screen?
Refer to a slide, a handout, or questions	
Go to a new topic or person	
End the presentation	

Vocabulary notebook

See page 71.

2 Grammar Expectations, necessity, requests, etc.

Figure it out

A How does the speaker express the ideas below? Underline the sentences in the presentation. Then read the grammar chart.

1. I believe there's a handout going around.
2. The projector is unable to connect.
3. Can somebody turn the lights off?

Modal verbs

Grammar extra
See page 155.

Modal verbs can express a range of meanings. Here are some.

Expectations	*There* ***should / ought to*** *be a handout going around.*
Guesses	*The projector* ***must*** *be warming up. It* ***might / could / may*** *be broken.*
Necessity	*I* ***should / ought to / have to / need to / 'd better*** *stop. ('d = had)*
Suggestions/advice	*You* ***might want to*** *check out the articles on the handout.*
Ability	***Can*** *you all see the screen?*
Failure (to operate)	*The projector* ***won't*** *connect to my laptop.*
Requests	***Could / Would / Can*** *somebody turn the lights off, please?*
Offers	***I'll*** *make the screen bigger. I* ***can / could*** *turn it up.*
Permission	***May* / Could / Can*** *I ask a question? Yes, you* ***may* / can.*** (*More formal)

B CD 2.29 **Circle the best modal verbs to complete the extracts from a presentation. Then listen and check.**

1. "OK, **can / would** you hear me at the back? Good. So, let's get started. You **could / should** all have a handout by now. Oh, wait – the projector **might not / won't** come on. It **might / ought to** be turned off. **May / Could** someone help me with it, please? Oh, it's not plugged in! Sorry. OK. So, **would / can** you see that clearly?"
2. "So, I'm sure you **need to / must** be wondering how clothes can have health benefits in the future. It **might / had better** be useful to play you something I heard on the radio. It's about hats that will turn hard when something hits them so they act like a helmet. So, I **need to / would** turn on the sound. Um, that **must / can** be the volume here. Oh, **I'd better / won't** turn it up. That's better. You **would / ought to** be able to hear at the back."
3. "So, let's move on. There are lots of fun possibilities, too. Simon, **may / would** I ask you to stand up, please? Thank you. Oh, you **might want to / would** turn around and face everyone. And **should / would** you show everyone your T-shirt? So, in the future, imagine T-shirts like this but with words or images that change color or react to music. Well, that's all I have time for. I **won't / have to** stop now. Does anyone have any questions or comments?"

C Group work **Prepare and give a short presentation on one of the topics below. Use six of the expressions you learned from page 64. Share the best ideas with the class.**

The future of . . .

clothing   shopping   money

Lesson C *I would think . . .*

1 Conversation strategy Softening opinions

A **Which do you enjoy more: going to the movies or watching movies at home?**

B CD 2.30 **Listen. What does Harry think about the future of movie theaters?**

Chris Wow! There's almost no one here tonight.

Tina Yeah. You know, I wonder if we'll still be going to the movies in ten years.

Harry Oh, I think so.

Tina I don't know. I'd say we probably won't. It's easier to watch movies at home – cheaper, too.

Harry Yeah, but going to the movies is different. It's more social.

Chris And it's a great first date. That's not going to change, is it?

Harry I hope not. I would think that movie theaters will find ways to attract more people . . .

Tina I guess so. But like what?

Harry Well, things that make movies more realistic, like seats that move . . .

Tina Ugh. I get motion sickness.

Chris And gaming. And you'll be able to choose how the movie ends.

Harry Yeah. I would imagine people will always want to go to the movies, but it'll be a different experience.

C **Notice** how Tina and Harry use *would* or *'d* to soften their opinions. Find examples in the conversation.

I would say . . . ***I'd say . . .***
I would think . . . ***I'd think . . .***
I would imagine . . .

In conversation . . .

People mostly say: *I would say, I would think,* and *I'd say.*

About you

D CD 2.31 **Listen to the opinions below. Complete each one with the softening expression you hear. Then discuss the opinions with a partner. Which do you agree with?**

1. ______________ the whole experience is better at a theater. You get better sound, and the screen's bigger. At home I sometimes fall asleep during a movie.
2. ______________ there'll be even more movies in 3D, because people like to feel part of the action.
3. ______________ theaters will stay popular. People like to go out with their friends.
4. ______________ theaters are not going to disappear anytime soon. But they're going to have to come up with some exciting innovations to stay in business.
5. ______________ people would enjoy choosing the ending to a movie. It'd be fun.
6. ______________ that we won't go to theaters in the future. We'll have the technology at home.

2 Strategy plus *I think so.*

CD 2.32 You can use ***I think so*** or ***I don't think so*** as a response. Don't use *I think* or *I don't think* as a response.

You can also use these responses.
I guess so or *I guess not.*
I hope so or *I hope not.*

In conversation . . .

I think so and *I don't think so* are the most common of these responses.

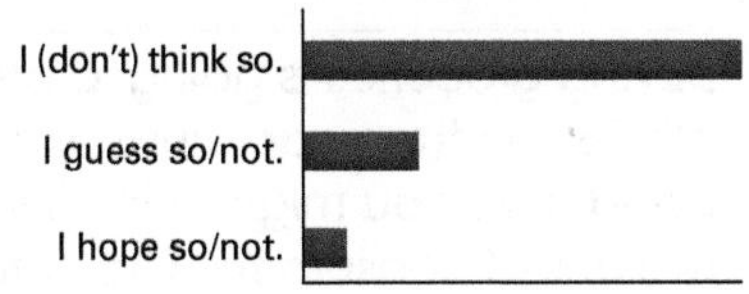

A Complete the conversations with appropriate responses from above. Then practice the conversations with a partner.

1. *A* Do you think going to the movies will be a very different experience in the future?
   B _______ . I mean, you'll still be watching a movie.
2. *A* Do you think that one day there'll be no actors at all, and they'll all be computer generated?
   B _______ . We'll always want to see real people in movies.
3. *A* Do people enjoy going to movie theaters just because it's something they can do with friends?
   B _______ . It's always fun to talk about the movie afterwards.
4. *A* Would you enjoy gaming in a movie theater?
   B _______ . It'd be fun to play with a theater full of people.
5. *A* Do you think people will stay home more to play virtual-reality games and stuff?
   B _______ . You don't always feel like going out to a theater in the evening.

About you **B** Pair work **Ask and answer the questions in Exercise A. Give your own answers.**

3 Listening and strategies Future entertainment

A CD 2.33 **Listen to four conversations about entertainment in the future. What four topics do the people talk about? Number the topics below 1–4. There is one extra topic.**

Topic	Agree	Disagree
_____ live music		
_____ reading		
_____ theater		
_____ travel		
_____ virtual-reality games		

B CD 2.34 **Listen again. Do the speakers agree? Check (✓) the correct columns in the chart above.**

About you **C** Group work **Discuss the five topics above. What do you think will happen in the future?**

A Well, I would think we'll still have books – even in 20 years. Don't you?
B Actually, I don't think so. I'd imagine we'll all be reading books on our computers or . . .

Lesson D *Future news*

1 Reading

A **Prepare** **Look at these headings from an article. What do you think the article is about?**

a. Miracle cures!
b. High-tech checkouts on the way!
c. Warmer, wetter, and more extremes!
d. More intelligent than a human!

B **Read for main ideas** **Read the article. Write the headings above the correct sections of the article.**

What does the future look like?

1 ______________________

Buying groceries is going to be much more efficient in the near future, experts say. "Thank goodness," you might think, if you're one of the millions of consumers who hate to set foot in a supermarket. Retailers predict that computerized shopping carts will be directing us to different areas of a store, based on our shopping lists. (That's the shopping list you'll be downloading from your smartphone as you enter the store.) Touch-screen terminals in each section of the store will give you access to any information you need. If you want a recipe, you'll be able to print one out. If you want to find out where produce comes from or its nutritional value, you'll be able to get that information, too. Then when you get to the self-checkout, "smart scales" will recognize all your produce by sight, weigh it, and price it. These developments should eventually make shopping a much quicker and easier process.

2 ______________________

If scientists are correct, our weather is going to change dramatically in the next century, which will affect us in a number of ways. Climatologists say our climate will get warmer and wetter, and that we're going to experience flooding on a huge scale, as rising temperatures cause icecaps to melt and sea levels to rise. But what will the impact of climate change be? Islands and even whole countries might ultimately disappear under water, which could create millions of refugees and migrants, as people seek new homes. Economists say climate change will also affect coastal industries, such as tourism and fishing, while ecologists predict that thousands of plants and animals may well become extinct. The effects of climate change will likely be considerable.

Reading tip

Writers use different ways to address the reader, including *you*, *we*, *everyone*, and *people*.

3 ______________________

There's a much brighter future for the victims of accidents, and particularly those who have lost arms or legs. Inventors are already perfecting artificial limbs that can perform in much the same way as human limbs. Transplants might eventually become much more common than now. Already surgeons are attempting risky arm transplants. But imagine the more distant future, when scientists may not need to perform such surgeries and might, instead, be able to treat a patient with medicines that enable arms and legs to grow back. Accident victims in the future will certainly have more treatment options.

4 ______________________

The future of artificial intelligence is exciting. According to computer engineers, you won't need to type words into a search engine in the future. Instead, you'll be able to talk to your computer, ask it questions, and get immediate answers. It will also remember all your conversations so that it can give more precise help the next time you ask. One day your computer will even give you advice, or act as a therapist! Imagine that – everyone will have their own personal therapist right on their laptop! Speaking to computers will certainly change the relationship we have with them.

C React Look back at the article, and write notes about the items below. Then compare with a partner.

- two things you learned from the article
- something you already knew or had heard
- the development you think would be most useful
- the most interesting piece of news you read
- the change you feel is the least likely
- the best and the worst piece of news

2 Focus on vocabulary Nouns for people

A Find the words from the box in the article on page 68. Then use the words to complete the questions.

✓ climatologists	inventors	retailers
consumers	migrants	therapists
ecologists	refugees	victims
economists		

1. What major changes do climatologists predict in the weather?
2. According to __________, how will a change in climate affect plants and animals?
3. Why will climate change create millions of __________ and __________?
4. What industries might be affected by climate change, according to __________?
5. What kinds of changes might __________ make in their stores in the future?
6. How will that improve the shopping experience for __________?
7. What have __________ created to help __________ of accidents?
8. Do you think computers will make good __________? Would you take advice from one?

B Pair work Ask and answer the questions in Exercise A. Use information from the article and any other information you know. Are there any areas where you do not agree?

"One thing climatologists predict is that we're going to get more flooding. Actually, there have been some terrible floods this year."

3 Viewpoint Is it for the better or worse?

A Group work Choose three topics from the list below. What changes might there be in these areas in the future? Will they be for the better or worse? Discuss your ideas.

- education
- work
- technology in the home
- family life
- food
- the media
- medicine
- the climate
- computer software

In conversation . . .

You can use these expressions to quote information you've heard.

Apparently, / Evidently, . . .
They say . . .
I've heard / read . . .

A *I would say that education will be very different. I mean, they say there might not even be school buildings in the future.*

B *Yes. Apparently, there are already some schools that exist only online.*

B Class activity Take turns telling your ideas to the class. Vote on whether you think each idea will happen and if the change will be for the better.

Writing *Future living*

In this lesson, you . . .

- structure a paragraph.
- use modal verbs with adverbs.
- avoid errors with adverbs.

Task Write a short article.

How will everyday life be different in the future? Will it be better?

A Look at a model **Read the paragraph. Do you agree with the writer? Underline the topic sentence, number the supporting sentences, and check (✓) the concluding sentence.**

One aspect of life that will certainly be very different and better in the future is education. It will likely become more personalized, and students might well follow individual programs. Students will probably spend less time in class and more time studying online at their own pace. The traditional classroom will eventually disappear, and college buildings may well become obsolete because people will be able to study at home. As a result, education will undoubtedly be more motivating and effective. Studying will ultimately change and be a more rewarding experience for each individual student.

Paragraphs

Paragraphs sometimes have these parts:

- **a topic sentence,** which gives the main idea.
- **supporting sentences,** which give reasons, examples, or explanations to support the main idea.
- **a concluding sentence,** which summarizes the paragraph.

B Focus on language **Circle seven more modal verbs with adverbs in the paragraph. Check the meaning of the adverbs. Then read the grammar chart.**

Modal verbs + adverbs in writing

Writers use adverbs after *will* to show how certain they are.
Inevitably, certainly, and *undoubtedly* add certainty.
*Education will **certainly** be different.*
Inevitably is often used for negative events.
*It will **inevitably** be difficult for some.*
Ultimately and *eventually* mean "certain after some time."
*Schools will **eventually** disappear.*
Likely and *probably* mean "fairly certain."
*Students will **probably** not sit in class.*
Writers use *well* after *may, might,* and *could* to mean "more certain."
*Schools may **well** become obsolete.*

Writing vs. Conversation

People use *may well* in formal writing and speaking.

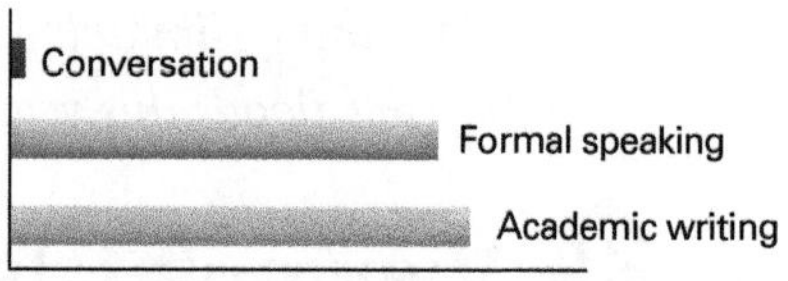

Common errors

Be careful with these adverbs.
Eventually does not mean "maybe."
Ultimately does not mean "recently."
Actually does not mean "now" – it means "in fact."
Currently means "now."

C **Rewrite the sentences using the adverbs given.**

1. Education will be more learner-oriented in the future. (certainly)
2. Students will study a wider range of subjects. (undoubtedly)
3. School buildings might become community centers. (well)
4. The idea of a school day will become obsolete. (eventually)
5. All college programs will be online. (likely)
6. Some students will have problems studying on their own. (inevitably)

D Brainstorm and write **Look back at the task at the top of the page. Brainstorm and organize ideas for your article. Then write a paragraph with a topic sentence, supporting sentences, and a concluding sentence. Use the adverbs in Exercise B.**

Vocabulary notebook *Present yourself!*

Learning tip **Idea strings**

When you learn a new expression, think of different ways you can use it. Create an "idea string" for it.

> I'll be talking about . . .
> the influence of television on young people. /
> the use of technology in schools.

A **Imagine you are giving a presentation. Use the expressions in the box to complete the "idea strings." Then add one more idea of your own.**

As you'll see . . .	I'll allow time for . . .	Let's . . .
Can you see . . .	I want to look at . . .	There should be . . .

1. ________ at the back? / the slide? / ________ ?
2. ________ a handout / a questionnaire / ________ going around.
3. ________ my research, / the future of transportation, / ________ .
4. ________ on the slide, / on your handout, / ________ , . . .
5. ________ questions / discussion / ________ at the end.
6. ________ get started, / move on, / ________ .

Let's . . .

The most common expressions with *Let's* in academic speaking are:
Let's see . . .
Let's say . . .
Let's look at . . .

B **Choose a topic for a presentation. Then complete these sentences with your own ideas.**

1. In this presentation, I want to look at ________ .
2. I'd like to begin by ________ .
3. Let's move on and look at ________ .
4. I'd better stop there and ________ .
5. I'll just conclude by saying ________ .
6. I'll turn it over to ________ .

C **Word builder** **Can you guess the meanings of these presentation expressions? Match each expression with its meaning. Write the letters a–h.**

1. I'll also touch on . . . ____
2. I'd like to draw your attention to . . . ____
3. We'll come back to that later. ____
4. I'll just skip over this next slide. ____
5. I'd like to introduce *(name)* . . . ____
6. To sum up, . . . ____
7. The next issue I want to address is . . . ____
8. Please feel free to interrupt and ask questions. ____

a. The next thing I want to talk about is . . .
b. I'll also talk briefly about . . .
c. I won't talk about this next slide.
d. Here is *(name)* . . .
e. We'll look at or talk about that later.
f. You can stop me if you have a question.
g. I want you to look at . . .
h. To summarize, . . .

On your own

Choose a topic and prepare a short presentation. Record yourself. Then listen and count how many expressions you used from page 64.

Checkpoint 2 *Units 4–6*

1 Words for work

About you

A Complete the sentences with verbs. Which are the five most important pieces of advice? Discuss with a partner, using *would* / *'d* to soften your opinions.

How to get a promotion at work

1. Follow your boss's advice.
2. _________ some training to _________ new skills.
3. _________ interest in getting a promotion.
4. Say how you can _________ the company money.
5. Always _________ the goals your manager sets.
6. _________ progress with projects and _________ deadlines.
7. _________ an application when there's a new position.
8. Don't be afraid to _________ competition from colleagues.

"I'd say it's important to follow your boss's advice – it might help you get a promotion."

About you

B Write sentences about your future career. Start your sentences with these expressions and a verb. Then compare ideas with a partner.

1. I think I'm going to be . . .
2. I'll probably be . . .
3. When I . . .
4. I might . . .
5. Before this class . . .
6. I may be . . .

"I think I'm going to be studying for another four years if I get accepted at grad school."

2 Wishes, hopes, and regrets

A Circle the correct verb forms to complete the conversations. Then practice with a partner.

1. *A* So, when you look back on last year, do you wish you **'d done** / **did** anything differently?
   B Yeah. I suppose. Like, I wish I **didn't spend** / **hadn't spent** so much last semester. You know, if I hadn't bought so many clothes and things, I **wouldn't be** / **wasn't** in debt now.
2. *A* What **would** / **will** you change about your city if you had the opportunity?
   B Well, I wish we **can** / **could** do something about the subway. I mean, I wish the trains **weren't** / **aren't** so crowded. And I wish people **don't** / **wouldn't** throw trash on them.
3. *A* If someone **had offered** / **would offer** you a job last year, would you **have taken** / **take** it?
   B As a matter of fact, I was offered a job. And I **might take** / **might have taken** it if it had been a really good job, but it wasn't. But if I had taken it, I **wouldn't be** / **weren't** in this class now. I just **wish** / **hope** I'll get a job next year.
4. *A* If you **can** / **could** raise money for a charity, which charity would you choose?
   B Well, if I **had to** / **would have to** choose a charity, I'd probably choose one for kids. In fact, I donated money to one last year. I hope it **made** / **would make** a difference.

About you

B Pair work **Take turns asking and answering the questions in Exercise A. Use *as a matter of fact* or *in fact* to give or correct information.**

A So, do you wish you'd done anything differently last year?
B I suppose. As a matter of fact, I wish I'd spent more time with my family.

3 The state of the world

A Fill in the blanks with the words in the box. Then circle the correct options to complete the sentences.

distribution	eradicate	polluted	protection	unemployment
environmental	✓ investment	poverty	starvation	wealth

1. Investment in education is expensive, but it saves **the money / money** eventually. **Education / The education** is crucial because educated people are less likely to live below the ________ level.
2. Research **show / shows** that 10 percent of the population owns over 70 percent of the ________.
3. People are more likely to be sick if there's **a pollution / pollution.** ________ air affects your health.
4. In areas of high ________, over 25 percent of people don't have **a job / job.** You often find that people suffer from **the mental illnesses / mental illnesses** in these areas.
5. In **the / a** world today, 925 million people don't have enough to eat. We really need to do more to ________ hunger or ________. The ________ of food should be more efficient.
6. If you are interested in the ________ of the environment, buy **the cotton / cotton** that is organic. There is **an / some** evidence that growing cotton causes serious ________ damage.

About you

B Pair work **Discuss the information in Exercise A. What ideas do you have for solutions? Use *I suppose* when you're not 100 percent sure and adverbs to show your attitude toward what you say.**

"I suppose investment in education is important. Clearly, it changes lives."

4 Prepare and present yourself

A Circle the best modal verbs. Then write in appropriate responses with *think*, *guess*, and *hope* to complete the conversation.

A Hey, Bob. **Can / Will** I ask you a question? Do you have a minute?

B Um, I guess so. I've got a class at ten, but I **should / need to** have a few minutes. What is it?

A Well, I have a second interview for a job tomorrow, and I really **will / should** get ready for it. I **need to / may** think about what to ask, you know, about salary or benefits and stuff.

B Yeah. You **can / ought to** think about what you want. You **might want to / 'll** make a list.

A OK. **Would / May** you help me? I've got my laptop. Oh, it **won't / shouldn't** turn on.

B You**'d better / won't** plug it in. OK, so let's see . . . Do they provide health insurance?

A Oh, ________. They **must / might want to** have it. Don't all companies offer some help with insurance?

B ________. Not all of them do. And ask, "**Can / Might** I work from home?" Do they allow it?

A ________. I know some people do. Oh, and they **should / had better** offer training.

B How many presentation expressions can you add to the word webs?

Today I want to look at . . .

Start or end a presentation

Introduce or change a topic

Refer to a slide, a handout, or questions

C Pair work **Prepare a presentation on the ideal company. What benefits would it offer? Use *what if . . . ?*, *suppose*, and *imagine* to suggest possible ideas.**

"Today I want to look at the ideal employer. Imagine a company that gives you 12 weeks vacation."

3 Unit 1, Lesson B Questions with answers

Sometimes people ask an information question and then suggest one or more answers to it. Notice the intonation.

*How often do you tend to use **email**? Every **day**?*

*When do you update your **profile**? At **night**? On the **weekends**?*

A CD 1.05 **Read and listen to the information above. Repeat the example questions.**

About you

B CD 1.06 **Listen and repeat these questions. Then ask and answer the questions with a partner.**

1. Who do you generally text? Your family?
2. What topics do you avoid discussing online? Politics? Religion?
3. What personal information do you put online? Your phone number?
4. How much of your social life do you organize online? Like, all of it?
5. What do you think is the best way to end a relationship? Send a text?

About you

C Pair work **Change partners and ask the questions in Exercise B again, suggesting a different answer. Continue each conversation.**

A *Who do you generally text? Your friends?*
B *Um, yeah. I mostly text my friends. I guess I tend to call my family. How about you?*

4 Unit 2, Lesson A *which* clauses

Notice how a *which* clause has a slight pause before it. When a *which* clause ends what you say, it often has a falling intonation.

*I bet celebrities hate seeing bad photos of themselves, **which probably happens a lot**.*

*People always want to know everything about their lives, **which must be difficult**.*

A CD 1.17 **Read and listen to the information above. Repeat the example sentences.**

B CD 1.18 **Listen and repeat these sentences about celebrities.**

1. Photographers are always following celebrities around, which must be a pain.
2. The magazines make up all these stories about them, which is probably annoying.
3. People complain about them even when they do charity work, which is totally unfair.
4. They can't have a private life – even their breakups are in the news, which must be awkward.
5. People expect them to live perfect lives, which is impossible.
6. There are websites that tell you where celebrities are, which must be scary for them.

About you

C Pair work **Discuss the sentences in Exercise B. Which ones do you agree with?**

A *I agree with the first sentence. It seems like photographers are always taking pictures of celebrities, which must be annoying for them.*
B *I know. Some photographers will do anything to get good pictures, which really isn't right.*

4 Unit 3, Lesson B Auxiliary verbs

Notice how the speakers reduce *Did you* and *Had you*.

***Did you* can be one or two syllables.**

Did you *struggle with any classes last semester?*

What ***did you*** *do about it?*

***Had you* is always two syllables.**

Had you *heard the expression "Life's too short" before this class?*

Where ***had you*** *heard it?*

A CD 1.31 **Read and listen to the information above. Repeat the example questions.**

B CD 1.32 **Listen and repeat these questions.**

1. Did you hear from anyone out of the blue last year? Who did you hear from?
2. Had you heard the expression "Truth is stranger than fiction" before this class? Where had you heard it?
3. Did you struggle with English when you first started learning it? Why did you find it difficult?
4. Had you been studying English for very long before you started this class? How long had you been studying?
5. Did you miss any classes last year? How many did you miss?
6. Did you learn anything from the life lessons you read about in this lesson? What did you learn?

About you

C Class activity **Ask your classmates the first question in each pair of questions in Exercise B. When you find someone who answers "yes," ask information questions to find out more details.**

A Did you hear from anyone out of the blue last year?
B Actually, yeah I did.
A So, who did you hear from?

4 Unit 4, Lesson A Word stress

Some words are stressed on the first syllable.		Some are stressed on the second or third syllable.			
■ ▪	■ ▪ ▪	▪ ■	▪ ■ ▪	▪ ■ ▪ ▪	▪ ▪ ■ ▪
deadline	*interview*	*advice*	*employer*	*experience*	*information*

A CD 2.03 **Read and listen to the information above. Repeat the example words.**

About you

B CD 2.04 **Listen. Underline the stressed syllable in the words in bold. Then ask and answer the questions with a partner.**

1. Would you like to work in **management**? Do you have any **experience** in managing people?
2. How's your **knowledge** of English? Is there **evidence** you need English to get a job?
3. Have you ever submitted an **application** for a new job or a **promotion**?
4. Have you decided on a **career** yet? How much **competition** is there for jobs in that field?
5. Are you making **progress** in your studies or work? Have you had any **feedback**?
6. How much do you know about **computers**?
7. Do you have to meet **deadlines**? Is your **employer** or **professor** very strict about them?
8. What's the best way to prepare for an **interview**? What **information** should you know about the job?

4 Unit 5, Lesson B Shifting word stress

Notice that some words in the same word family are stressed on a different syllable.

environment *environmental*

eradicate *eradication*

Some words are stressed on the same syllable.

pollute *pollution*

invest *investment*

A CD 2.16 **Read and listen to the information above. Repeat the example words.**

B CD 2.17 **Listen to these pairs of words. Are the words stressed on the same (S) or a different (D) syllable? Write S or D. Practice saying these words.**

1. starving – starvation _____
2. create – creation _____
3. unemployed – unemployment _____
4. education – educate _____
5. distribute – distribution _____
6. economy – economic _____

About you

C Group work **If you represented a global charity, which of these issues would be your priorities? Discuss the ideas, then number the issues 1–7 (1 = highest priority, 7 = lowest priority).**

- *End starvation.* Approximately one-third of the world's population is starving. _____
- *Educate every child.* Millions of kids don't go to school because they must work. _____
- *Stop polluting water, air, and soil.* Pollution causes 40 percent of world deaths. _____
- *Eradicate poverty.* Its eradication would give half the world's children better lives. _____
- *Invest in new jobs.* Investment in new jobs helps the economy and leads to economic growth. _____
- *Protect animals and plants.* Better environmental protection could save thousands of species. _____

4 Unit 6, Lesson A Silent consonants

Notice how some consonants are "silent" and not pronounced.

l → *could, walk, half*	*th* → *clothes**	*k* → *know*
gh → *ought, light*	*h* → *hour, exhausted*	*p* → *psychology*
g → *design*	*t* → *listen*	*n* → *column*
b → *debt*		

* Some speakers pronounce the ***th*** in *clothes*.

A CD 2.26 **Read and listen to the information above. Repeat the example words.**

B CD 2.27 **Read these sentences. Draw a line (/) through the silent consonants in the words in bold. Then listen, check, and repeat.**

1. *A* **Could** you turn off the **lights**, please, so we can see the screen?
   B Oh, **right**. Hey, **listen**. Maybe we **should** close the blinds, too.
2. *A* Do you think **clothes** will be different in the future?
   B Oh, there's no **doubt** about that. We **might** even have clothes that heat up and everything.
3. *A* Are you interested in **design**? I mean, **could** you name any fashion **designers**?
   B I **know** a couple of **foreign** designers, but to be **honest**, I'm not really into fashion.
4. *A* Have you read anything about the **psychology** of shopping online?
   B Not much. **Though half** my friends spend **hours** shopping online. One even got into **debt** because of it. He **talks** about it a lot.

About you

C Pair work **Practice the conversations. Then practice again, giving your own answers.**

Questions

	Information questions	*Yes-No* questions
present of *be*	*How**'s** your English class this year?*	***Is** it fun?*
past of *be*	*Where **was** your mother born?*	***Were** both your parents born here?*
simple present	*How often **do** your parents **call** you?*	***Does** everyone in your family **have** a cell phone?*
simple past	*What time **did** you **get up** today?*	***Did** you **get up** early?*
present continuous	*Why **are** you **studying** English?*	***Are** you **studying** English for your job?*
past continuous	*Where **were** you **living** in 2010?*	***Were** you **living** here?*
present perfect	*Which cities **have** you **been** to?*	***Has** your family ever **lived** abroad?*
present perfect continuous	*How long **have** you **been studying** English?*	***Have** you **been studying** English for a long time?*
modal verbs	*What **should** you **say** no to more often?*	***Can** you **say** no to chocolate?*

- *Who* and *What* can be the subject of an information question. They take a singular verb.
  ***Who** sits next to you in class?*
  ***What** made you decide to study English?*
- The subject can also be a question word + noun. The verb agrees with the noun.
  ***What word** describes you best?*
  ***Which cities** are the most beautiful?*

A Complete the questions. Use the forms on the left with the verbs in parentheses.

present of *be*
1. Where ________ your family from originally? (be)
2. ________ your parents from another city? (be)

past of *be*
3. What ________ your favorite game when you were little? (be)
4. ________ you good at sports as a child? (be)

simple present
5. How many people ________ you ________ in your neighborhood? (know)
6. ________ your best friend ________ near you? (live)
7. Which friend ________ the most time at your house? (spend)
8. What ________ you and your friends ________ on the weekend? (do)

simple past
9. When ________ you ________ home last night? (get)
10. ________ you ________ with your friends last night? (go out)

present continuous
11. What ________ you ________ for exercise now? (do)
12. ________ you ________ enough exercise these days? (get)

past continuous
13. What ________ you ________ at this time yesterday? (do)
14. ________ you ________ with your friends yesterday? (hang out)

present perfect
15. How long ________ you ________ your best friend? (know)
16. ________ your best friend ever ________ you angry? (make)

present perfect continuous
17. How ________ your English class ________ ________ this year? (go)
18. ________ you ________ ________ a lot? (learn)

modal verbs
19. ________ you ________ English better than your friends? (can / speak)
20. In your opinion, how much time ________ you ________ practicing English every day? (should / spend)

About you

B Write your own answers to the questions. Give as much information as you can.

My father is originally from Ecuador and my mother was born in Bolivia, but we live in Colombia now. My sisters and I were all born here.

1 Frequency expressions

- In the simple present, frequency adverbs usually go after the subject in affirmative statements and after *don't* and *doesn't* in negative statements. In the present continuous, they go after *am, is, are (not).*
  My sister ***rarely*** *uses email.* *She doesn't* ***often*** *use a computer.*
  My kids are ***constantly*** *texting.* *They're not* ***always*** *talking on the phone.*
- Frequency adverbs usually go after modal verbs, although other patterns are possible.
  I'll ***usually*** *log on to my social network site after dinner.*
- These adverbs can go before the subject: *sometimes, usually, often, normally, generally, occasionally.*
  Occasionally *my son will email a family member.*
- Longer expressions often go at the end of a sentence: *once / twice a day, all the time, every once in a while.*
  We talk on the phone ***twice a week****.*

Common errors

Don't put an adverb between a verb and its object.
I ***often*** *check my email late at night.* (NOT ~~*I check often my email.*~~)

About you

Add the words and expressions to the sentences. Then rewrite the sentences so they are true for you.

1. I make phone calls. (never / after 10:00 p.m.) I never make phone calls after 10:00 p.m.
   Occasionally I make phone calls after 10:00 p.m.
2. My dad will text me. (occasionally / during his lunch break) ____________
3. My sister checks her email. (normally / before breakfast) ____________
4. I send personal letters. (rarely / these days) ____________
5. I instant message my friends. (generally / late at night) ____________
6. My best friend is sending me text messages. (constantly / during the day) ____________

2 State verbs

- In general, use these verbs in the simple form – not the continuous form – when they describe states: *agree, believe, know, mean, like, love, hate, look, seem, feel, sound, understand.*
  I ***know*** *I* ***don't need*** *a new phone, but I really* ***want*** *a red one.*
  "He ***doesn't seem*** *happy." "I* ***agree****. He* ***looks*** *a little upset today."*
  What kind of music ***do*** *you* ***like****?* (NOT ~~*What kind of music are you liking?*~~)
- Some verbs have a different meaning in the simple and continuous forms: *have, see, think.*
  Do *you* ***have*** *any children?* BUT ***Are*** *you* ***having*** *a nice time?* (at a party)
  I ***see*** *the problem.* BUT ***I'm seeing*** *someone right now.*
  What ***do*** *you* ***think*** *of this class?* BUT *You look happy. What* ***are*** *you* ***thinking*** *about?*

In conversation . . .

People often use *love* and *like* in the continuous to talk about news.
*"****I'm loving*** *my new job."*

A Complete the questions with the verbs given. Use the simple present or present continuous.

1. What ________ the word *eccentric* ________? (mean)
2. ________ you ________ that you can make new friends through a social network? (believe)
3. What ________ you ________ about right now? (think)
4. ________ everyone in your family ________ how to send text messages? (know)
5. ________ your parents ________ profiles on a social network? (have)

About you

B Write your own answers to the questions. Give as much information as you can.

Verbs in subject and object relative clauses

- In relative clauses, *who, that,* and *which* can be the subject or object of the verb. Use a singular verb with a singular subject and a plural verb with a plural subject.

	Subject relative clauses			
		subject	verb	object
Defining	*There's a TV show*	***that***	***arranges***	*plastic surgery.*
	TV shows	***that***	***arrange***	*plastic surgery **are** often criticized by doctors.*
Non-defining	*Celebrity magazines, **which need** to attract readers, **publish** some incredible stories.*			
	*My brother, **who** **loves** celebrity gossip, **reads** celebrity magazines all the time.*			

	Object relative clauses			
		object	subject	verb
Defining	*People read about the clothes*	(***that***)	*celebrities*	***wear.***
	I'm interested in the people	(***who / that***)	*my favorite actor*	***dates.***
Non-defining	*Reality shows, **which** I never watch, by the way, **have** millions of viewers.*			

- *Which* clauses that comment on a previous clause can be subject or object relative clauses. As a subject, *which* takes a singular verb.
  *Celebrity magazines sometimes invent stories, **which is** pretty shocking.*
  *Some people believe everything they read, **which** I find very scary.*

Common errors

Don't repeat the subject or object in a relative clause.
The actor who was on TV last week has . . . (NOT ~~*The actor who he was on TV last week has*~~ . . .)
The actor (that) I saw on TV last week has . . . (NOT ~~*The actor (that) I saw him on TV last week has*~~ . . .)

Complete the sentences with a singular or plural form of the verbs in parentheses.

1. In some cities, you can go on a "celebrity bus tour," which _________ (take) you through the neighborhoods of famous people and _________ (show) you their houses.
2. A celebrity who _________ (want) to avoid photographers _________ (have to) keep his or her plans secret.
3. Someone who _________ (be) obsessed with a celebrity often _________ (try) to look like that person.
4. Famous people who _________ (prefer) to protect their privacy _________ (try) to keep photographers away from their homes.
5. A photographer who _________ (chase) a celebrity in a car _________ (be) just reckless.
6. Celebrities often appear on talk shows, which _________ (not pay) them very much but _________ (give) them valuable publicity.
7. Fashion designers, who _________ (need) publicity, often _________ (lend) actors clothes to wear on TV.
8. One popular fashion designer, who _________ (work) a lot with celebrities, often _________ (lend) people her clothes to wear on TV.
9. Actors who _________ (get) arrested often _________ (use) the publicity, which just _________ (show) that "There's no such thing as bad publicity."

1 Using *that* clauses

- You can use different nouns with *that* clauses to present a point, such as a problem, or a fact, etc. You can omit *that* in speaking, but in general include *that* in your formal writing.
  The problem is
  The fact / reality is *that children watch too much television.*
  The point / thing is

  The ***biggest / main problem is*** *that children who watch too much TV can become overweight.*
  The ***odd / amazing thing is*** *that kids who watch too much TV are often aggressive at school.*

- You can add more information to *problem* or *thing* by using preposition + noun or + *-ing* form.
  The problem ***with watching too much television*** *is that it keeps you from getting exercise.*
  The worst thing ***about TV*** *these days is that kids watch it while they're eating.*

Writing vs. Conversation

Avoid using *The thing is . . .* in formal writing.

Rewrite these sentences by introducing them with the information in parentheses.

1. Kids can learn about current events by watching TV. (That's one good thing.)
   One good thing is that kids can learn about current events by watching TV.
2. Very young children learn a lot from watching educational programs. (That's the reality.)
3. Some children learn more about history from television than at school. (That's the interesting thing.)
4. They don't care about the shows their children watch. (That's the problem with parents today.)

2 *what* clauses

- You can use *what* clauses to emphasize a point as an opinion.
  Children are spending more and more time in front of the TV. This is surprising / clear. →
  What's surprising / clear *is that children are spending more and more time in front of the TV.*
  Children see a lot of violence on TV. That bothers me. →
  What bothers me *is that children see a lot of violence on TV.*

In conversation . . .

These *what* clauses are common ways of making a point.
What I'm saying is that . . .
What I'm trying to say is that . . .

A Rewrite these sentences by starting them with a *what* clause that gives the information in parentheses.

1. Television keeps children from getting enough exercise. (That bothers me.)
   What bothers me is that . . .
2. Children need to play and be creative, too. (That's what I'm saying.)
3. Kids watch a lot of violent TV shows, and that can make them aggressive. (That's really scary.)
4. Even educational TV shows prevent kids from exercising. (That's clear.)

About you

B Write down five of your own ideas about the influence of television on children. Use the expressions in the box to introduce your ideas.

The biggest problem with watching television is . . . The good thing about television is . . .
The point is . . . What bothers me is . . . What I'm trying to say is . . .

Time expressions with the simple past and present perfect

• You can use time expressions like these with the simple past to indicate a completed time in the past.		• You can use time expressions like these with the present perfect to indicate a "time up to now" which is not yet complete.	
I worked on a farm . . .		*I've had a lot of problems . . .*	
yesterday. *last week.* *in the fall.* *earlier this year.* *right after college.*	*the year before last.* *a couple of years ago.* *at the end of July.* *when I was 20.*	*lately.* *so far.* *to date.* *in my life.* *up until now.*	*over the past few years.* *in the last few days.* *since last year.* *since we last spoke.*

- You can use some time expressions with both the simple past and the present perfect:
  today, this week / month / year, for (quite) a while, for a long time, recently.
  We had some bad luck this year. (The speaker is referring to a point in the past.)
  We've had some bad luck this year. (The speaker sees this year as a period of time up to now.)
  We've been busy recently. (The speaker may not be busy now but considers this relevant now.)

- Time expressions usually go at the beginning or end of a statement.
  ***Yesterday** I ran into an old friend.* OR *I ran into an old friend **yesterday**.*

- Use *for* with a period of time. Use *since* with a phrase or a clause which gives a point in time.
  *I've lived here **for** many years / **since** 1995 / **since** I was a child.*

Common errors

- Don't put a time expression between the verb and the object.
  *We bought a new television **last week**.* (NOT ~~*We bought last week a new television*~~.)
- Avoid putting the time expressions above (except *recently*) between the subject and the verb.
  *She got married **right after college**.* (NOT ~~*She right after college got married*~~.)

A Complete the sentences with the simple past or present perfect of the verbs in parentheses.

1. My sister moved (move) to Chicago earlier this year, and so far things have gone (go) pretty well for her. What's great is that she ________ (find) a job right after she got there.
2. My parents ________ (travel) a lot over the past few years. To date they ________ (visit) five different countries. The year before last, they ________ (take) a trip to South Africa.
3. I ________ (be) extremely busy in the last few days. I ________ (not have) a minute to take a break up until now.
4. My best friend ________ (have) some bad luck since he finished school. Last year, for example, he ________ (lose) his job, and he ________ (be) out of work for a long time. He has another job now, but the thing is that he ________ (not be) happy with it recently.
5. I ________ (be) pretty lucky since I got this job. The really amazing thing is that I ________ (get) two raises so far.
6. A lot of things ________ (happen) in my life since we last spoke. First of all, I ________ (meet) someone wonderful in the spring, and in fact we ________ (get) married just last month

About you

B Write four sentences about yourself or people you know. Use the ideas from above.

A new couple has just moved into the apartment next to us.

Time expressions with the past perfect

- You can use the following time expressions with the past perfect.

already / still / yet

*By the time I got to the restaurant, most people had **already** eaten.*
*When I left for class, I **still** hadn't completed my assignment, so I finished it on the bus.*
*My best friend hadn't arrived **yet**, but I couldn't wait any longer, so I went home.*

(not) until after

*I did**n't** find my watch **until after** I'd bought a new one.*

by the time

*I was exhausted **by the time** I'd finished cleaning the house.*

never . . . before

*She was a great teacher. I learned things that I'd **never** understood **before**.*

earlier / previously / years ago

*I got a stomachache from something I'd eaten **earlier**.*
*It was a problem I'd had **previously**, so I knew what caused it.*
*I knew exactly what to do because I'd seen a doctor about it **years ago**.*

A Complete the sentences with appropriate time expressions in the box.

by the time earlier never . . . before until after

1. Last summer I took a vacation in Australia. I didn't know much about the country because I'd ________ been there ________, but I was really excited about the trip.
2. A month before I left, things started to go wrong. I lost my camera, and I didn't find it ________ I'd bought a new one.
3. I finally found my old camera in my suitcase! I'd put it there ________ so I wouldn't forget it.
4. The week before the trip, my boss gave me an urgent project to complete. I was exhausted ________ I'd finished it.

already previously still yet

5. The day I left, I felt stressed because I ________ hadn't packed my suitcase. It took a long time to fit everything in.
6. A friend of mine drove me to the airport. He'd driven there a few times ________, so he thought he knew the way. But he got lost!
7. By the time I got to the gate, most of the passengers had ________ boarded the plane.
8. Luckily, they hadn't closed the gate ________, and I was able to get on the flight. In the end, everything worked out fine. I guess I learned that it almost always does!

About you

B Write 5–10 sentences about an interesting experience you've had. Use the past perfect and time expressions.

Last week I went to a new club. All my friends had already been there, but I hadn't . . .

1 Making uncountable nouns countable

- Uncountable nouns are often names of materials or of groups of things. You can use *a piece of* to refer to an example or a part of these uncountable nouns: *a piece of paper / plastic / clothing / jewelry / furniture / music / equipment / information / software / advice / evidence.*
  *Can I give you **a piece of advice**? When you buy **a new piece of equipment**, check the warranty.*
- With some uncountable nouns, you need to use a different countable noun to refer to an example or a part: *travel – trip; cash – coin* or *bill; feedback – comment; luggage – bag; work – job or position.*
  *My job includes a lot of international **travel**. I go on nine or ten business **trips** a year.*
  *My boss's **feedback** is very valuable. Her **comments** are always useful.*

Common errors

Use (*How*) *much* with uncountable nouns and (*How*) *many* with plural countable nouns.
Don't take ***too much luggage / too many bags***. (NOT . . . ~~*too many luggages*~~)
How much travel / How many trips *are you planning?* (NOT ~~*How many travels . . .*~~)

Complete the sentences with a countable noun like the uncountable noun in bold. Add *a, a piece of,* or *piece of* if necessary. Some have more than one answer.

1. Be sure to ask for **advice** before a job interview. Here's one important piece of advice: Only ask the interviewer questions that show your interest in the job.
2. If you're looking for rewarding **work**, think about applying for ________ in health care.
3. It's nice to have exercise **equipment** at home. One useful ________ is an exercise bike.
4. **Travel** can be expensive. When you plan ________, compare prices on the Internet.
5. Don't carry too much **luggage** when you travel. Just take one ________ with you.
6. Some **jewelry** is expensive, so before you buy ________, make sure it's something you like.

2 More about uncountable nouns

- Academic subjects and sports that end in *-s* are usually singular: *economics, genetics, mathematics, physics, politics; aerobics, gymnastics. News* also takes a singular verb.
  Physics was *my favorite subject in high school.*
  *The **news isn't** good, I'm afraid.*
- Some nouns are both countable and uncountable but they have different meanings, e.g. *business, competition, experience, paper, time, work.*
  *My mother has always worked in **business**. She has owned several **businesses**.*
  *I have a lot of **experience** using dangerous equipment. I've had some scary **experiences**.*

About you

Circle the correct words. Then write your own answers to the questions.

1. Are job candidates facing stiff **competition / competitions** these days?
2. Has it ever taken you **a long time / long time** to find a job?
3. Do you have **an experience / experience** preparing a résumé?
4. **Is / Are** mathematics a field that you're interested in?
5. **Do / Does** economics give people useful knowledge for a career in business?
6. Have you ever thought of starting **a business / business**?
7. Do you think that politics **interest / interests** young people as a career?
8. **Do / Does** the news ever depress you?

More about the definite article

- Use *the* with these common locations, especially after the prepositions *at* and *to*: *the office, the factory, the store, the mall, the gym, the library, the park, the pool, the post office, the bank.*
  I'd like to have exercise equipment ***at the office****. I never have time to go* ***to the gym****.*
  Some companies install ATMs so that employees don't have to go ***to the bank****.*

- Don't use *the* with these common locations, especially after the prepositions *at, to, in, before,* and *after: home, bed, work, school, college, class, prison, jail.*
  I arrive ***at work*** *early so that I can leave early to pick up my children* ***after school****.*
  Some companies offer special training programs for people who have been ***in prison****.*
  Many employees work during the day and go ***to college*** *at night.*

- Don't use *the* before meals. You can use an article when you describe a particular meal.
  I had ***breakfast*** *late, so I didn't eat much for* ***lunch****.*
  The lunch *we had at that new café wasn't very good. It was* ***an expensive lunch****, too.*

Common errors

It was late, so I went ***to bed****.* (NOT . . . *so I* ~~*went to the bed.*~~)
She couldn't go ***to work*** *because she was sick.* (NOT *She couldn't* ~~*go to the work . . .*~~)

A Complete these conversations with *the, a, an,* or (-) if no word is necessary.

1. *A* Around what time do you go to ___-___ bed at night?
   B Oh, I'm always in _________ bed by 10:00, because I have to be at _________ factory at 8.
2. *A* Did you have _________ breakfast this morning?
   B Yes, but I'm having _________ light lunch, because I'm going out for _________ expensive dinner.
3. *A* Have you ever wanted to take a nap after _________ big lunch?
   B Occasionally I'll do that at _________ home, but there's no place to sleep at _________ work.
4. *A* Do you do anything regularly for exercise, like go to _________ gym?
   B Well, sometimes I go for a run in _________ park, and every so often I go to _________ pool for a swim.
5. *A* Have you ever taken a pet with you to _________ work or to _________ school?
   B Actually, when I was in _________ college, a guy used to bring a pet rat to _________ class. The teacher never knew.
6. *A* Do you go straight home after _________ work?
   B Well, it seems like I always have something to do, like stop at _________ store to pick up something for _________ dinner or go to _________ bank for some cash.
7. *A* Do you ever do anything fun after _________ class, like go to a restaurant?
   B Um, sometimes I go out for _________ dinner with some classmates.
8. *A* Would you like to have flexible hours at _________ office?
   B Yeah, I'd like to be able to pick up my kids after _________ school.

About you

B Write your own answers to the questions above.

I usually go to bed around 10:30.

1 Continuous forms for conditions

- You can use past continuous forms to introduce hypothetical situations in the present.
  *If you **were hoping** to get a job with a charity, you might want to volunteer first.*
  *If you **were planning** to change the world, where would you start?*

- You can use past perfect continuous forms to introduce hypothetical situations in the past.
  *If the Salwens **had been living** in a small house, they wouldn't have been able to raise so much.*
  *Hannah might not have seen the homeless man if she **hadn't been looking** out the window.*

About you

Complete the questions with a continuous form of the verbs. Then answer the questions.

1. If you and your classmates ________ to raise money for a good cause, how would you do it? (try)
2. If you ________ so hard, what would you have done differently last year? (not work)
3. If you ________ about giving to a charity, what organization would you choose? Why? (think)
4. What would you do if you ________ down the street and you saw a homeless person? (walk)
5. If you ________ to help your community, what would you do? (plan)

2 *even if* and *unless* to talk about conditions

- You can use *even* to add special emphasis to a condition introduced by *if*.
  *I think I would give to charity **even if** I didn't have much money.*
  ***Even if** I had saved some money last year, I wouldn't have given it to a charity.*

- You can use *unless* to introduce what needs to happen or be true for something else to happen. It means "except if."
  *I wouldn't give money to charity **unless** I were a millionaire (**except if** I were a millionaire).*
  *= I would **only** give money to charity **if** I were a millionaire.*

- You can use the same verb forms with *even if* and *unless* as with *if* clauses.
  *I **wouldn't sell** my house unless it **were / was** really necessary.*
  *The Salwens **would have raised** money for charity even if Hannah **hadn't seen** the man that day.*

Common errors

Don't use ***unless*** when the event in the *if* clause actually happened.
***If they hadn't sold** their house, they wouldn't be as close now.* (NOT ~~*Unless they had sold . . .*~~)

About you

Complete the answers with the clauses in the box. More than one answer may be possible.

I didn't want them.	I had a very good job.	I had to put the donation on my credit card.
I only had a few things.	I wanted time off work.	I couldn't find a job when I got back.

1. *A* Would you give money to charity if you were out of work?
   B Absolutely. I would do it even if ________________
   C I don't think so. I would never do it unless ________________
2. *A* Would you ever give up a good position if you had a chance to spend a year traveling?
   B Sure. I wouldn't miss a chance like that unless ________________
   C Never. I wouldn't give up a good position even if ________________
3. *A* Would you give away your belongings if you had the chance to help someone?
   B I don't think so. I wouldn't give my things away unless ________________
   C Yes, I would. I'd give my things away even if ________________

1 Use of *wish* with *would*

- You can use *wish* followed by a clause with *would* in order to comment on a situation you would like to change.
  *You're always leaving the lights on! ➔ I **wish** you **wouldn't leave** the lights on.*
  *Why can't the kids spend less money on soda? ➔ I wish the kids **would spend** less money on soda.*
- You can comment on general situations using *people* or *they* in the clause with *would.*
  *I wish **they'd stop** tearing down the historic buildings in our neighborhood.*
  *I wish **people would learn** to recycle their bottles and cans.*

Common errors

Don't confuse *wish* and *hope.*
*I **hope** this information will be helpful to you.* (NOT ~~*I wish this information would be helpful to you.*~~)

A Comment on the situations below. Write sentences with *I wish* + a clause with *would*.

1. You use so much water! I wish you wouldn't use so much water!
2. You never recycle your newspapers. ______
3. Why don't people use public transportation more? ______
4. Why can't people be more polite on the bus? ______
5. They need to do something about water pollution. ______
6. People are always throwing their litter on the streets. ______

About you **B Write five sentences about situations you would like to change. Begin each sentence with *I wish* and include *would* or *wouldn't*.**

2 Strong wishes with *If only*

- You can use *If only* to introduce a strong wish, which is either difficult or impossible to achieve. The verb forms that follow *If only* are the same as those that follow *I wish.*
  *I wish people were more generous. ➔ **If only** people **were** more generous.*
  *I wish people would care about the homeless. ➔ **If only** people **would care** about the homeless.*
  *I wish we could predict the future. ➔ **If only** we **could predict** the future.*
- In writing, add a main clause to a sentence with *if only.*
  *If only people cared more about the homeless, **we might eradicate the problem**.*
  *If only we could predict the future, **we would all be a lot richer**.*

Common errors

Don't confuse *if only* and *only if.*
*I would miss work **only if** I were sick.* OR *I would **only** miss work **if** I were sick* (NOT ~~*I would miss work if only I were sick.*~~)

A Use *If only* to rewrite these thoughts as strong wishes. Some have more than one answer.

1. Why can't we find a way to end all wars? If only we could find a way to end all wars!
2. I don't know why people don't recycle more! ______
3. People are so narrow-minded about some things. ______
4. I wish we could predict natural disasters better. ______
5. I wish they would create more jobs for the unemployed. ______
6. I wish I hadn't quit my job. ______

About you **B Write five strong wishes of your own. Use *If only*.**

1 Plans and intentions with *be going to* and *will*

- You can use the future with *be going to* to talk about your plans or intentions when you have already made decisions. Use *will* for decisions you make at the moment of speaking.
  *I'**m going to be working** from home, so I'**m going to get** a laptop. I think **I'll look for** one today.*
- You can use *will* to state decisions in stores and restaurants, to offer help, or to make promises.
  *I'**ll take** this dress.* *I'**ll have** the fish.* *I'**ll open** the door.* *I **won't tell** anyone.*
- You can use the future continuous to tell people about plans that affect them or to go over plans you've agreed on. You can also use it to politely ask people about their own plans.
  *I'**ll be calling** you later.* (= We already agreed on this.) *I'**ll call** you later.* (= I just decided.)
  ***Will** you **be paying** with a credit card or a debit card?*

Common errors

Use *I'll* + verb to make an offer.
***I'll call** you tonight.* (NOT ~~*I call*~~ *you tonight.*)

Circle the most appropriate expressions. Say why you chose each expression.

It's a plan they've agreed on.

A Sorry to disturb you. I just wanted to remind you that **I'll be leaving / I'll leave** early tonight, like we agreed. **I'm going to take / I'll take** a friend out to dinner for her birthday.

B OK . . . Actually, it's Tuesday today, right? So **I'll leave / I'm going to be leaving** the office late tonight as usual. So . . . yeah, **I take care of / I'll take care of** anything that comes up.

A Thanks. So **I'm going to see / I'll see** you tomorrow morning, then.

B Well, tomorrow's busy. **Will you be coming in / Are you going to come in** at 8:00, as usual?

A If there's a lot to do, **I'm going to get / I'll get** here by 7:00. **I won't be / I'm not going to be** late, I promise.

2 Present forms in clauses that refer to the future

- Use the present in clauses that begin with *when, before, after, until,* or *as soon as* to refer to the future.
  ***Before** we **get to** the movie theater, I'm going to stop at an ATM. I'll need some cash **when** we **get** there.*
  *I won't be able to do anything **until** I **eat**. I'll buy something **as soon as** we **get** to the theater.*
- Use the present in clauses with *unless, as long as, so long as, providing (that),* and *provided (that)* that refer to the future. These expressions introduce something that needs to happen or be true so that something else can happen.
  *I can pay **as long as / so long as** we **go** to a café that takes debit cards.* OR *I can't pay **unless** we **go** . . .*
  *They won't charge interest **provided (that) / providing (that)** you **pay** the bill in full.*
- Use the present in clauses with *in case*, which introduces a possibility that you want to be ready for.
  *I'm going to take all my credit cards **in case** they **don't accept** one of them.*

About you

Combine the sentences using the words given. Then make three sentences true for you.

1. I'll lend you some money. You'll have to pay me back next week, though. (as long as)
   I'll lend you some money as long as you pay me back next week.
2. I'm not going to be taking a vacation next summer. I probably won't get a raise. (unless)
3. I won't be able to apply for a credit card right away. First, I'll need to get a full-time job. (until)
4. I'm going to take a lot of cash. They might not accept credit cards. (in case)
5. Our grocery store will give us a discount. We'll have to pay in cash, however. (provided that)

1 More on necessity modals

- You can use *should* (*not*), *ought* (*not*) *to*, and *had better* (*not*) to say what is advisable. Use *had better* in specific situations.
  *You **should / ought to** check the equipment before a presentation. You **shouldn't** begin until you check it.*
  *You'**d better** get going – it's almost 10:30. You'**d better not** be late for class again.*

- Use *must* (*not*) to say what is necessary. *Must* is mainly used in formal notices and announcements.
  *You **must** turn off your cell phone before the lecture. You **must not** use a cell phone during the lecture.*

- You can use *have to* and *need to* to say what is necessary in the affirmative. In the negative, however, these expressions are used to say what is NOT necessary.
  *You **have to / need to** carry a driver's license when you drive.* = It's necessary.
  *But you **don't have to / don't need to** carry your passport.* = It's not necessary.

About you

Complete the sentences with a modal form from the box. Often more than one answer is possible. Then write four sentences to describe rules or advice for your city.

need to	have to	must	'd better	should	ought to
don't need to	don't have to	must not	'd better not	shouldn't	

1. Here, the law says you must / have to / need to wear a helmet when you ride a motorcycle.
2. Many countries have a law that says you ______ wear a seat belt when you're riding in a car. Here, it's only necessary if you're sitting in the front seat – you ______ wear one in the back.
3. In many places, you ______ use your cell phone when you drive. It's against the law.
4. In most countries, you ______ stop your car for a flashing red light, but you ______ stop for a flashing yellow light. You ______ slow down, however.
5. You ______ look both ways before crossing a street. It's not a law, though.
6. We ______ go out tonight. There's going to be a big storm. We ______ stay home.

2 Possibility modals in the affirmative and negative

- Use *may (not), might (not),* and *must (not)* to make guesses. *Not* is generally not contracted.
  *We **may / might** have to end this meeting early.* = It's possible we'll have to . . .
  *We **may not / might not** have time for a lot of questions.* = It's possible we won't have time . . .
  *The principal isn't here. She **must** be busy today.* = It's likely she's . . .
  *The meeting is almost over. The principal **must not** be coming.* = It's likely she's not coming.

- You can also use *could* to talk about possibilities, but it often becomes *can't* in the negative and means "it's not possible."
  *The projector is brand new. It **can't be** broken.* = It's not possible that it's broken.
  *But it **could be** unplugged.* = It's possible that it's unplugged.

Circle the appropriate modal verbs in the sentences.

1. The elevator's not working. I'm afraid we **might** / **must** have to use the stairs.
2. My camera won't turn on. I suppose the battery **could** / **can** need recharging. Wait a minute. It simply **might not** / **can't** be the battery. I just recharged it last night!
3. My oven's not working. I **may not** / **can't** be able to get it fixed. I **might** / **must** need a new one.
4. My sister's not answering her cell phone. I think she **might not** / **could** have her cell phone with her. Or maybe the battery **could** / **must not** be dead. Or her phone **may not** / **must** be on.

Illustration credits

11: (cartoon) Liza Donnelly; **20:** (podcast icon) hleib/Shutterstock; **27:** (cartoon) Liza Donnelly; **29:** (flip pad) Jupiter Images/Getty Images; **36:** (cartoon) Liza Donnelly; **39:** (datebook) AXL/Shutterstock; **48:** (cartoon) Liza Donnelly; **60:** (background) CGTextures; **69:** (cartoon) Liza Donnelly

Photography credits

10: (top right from left to right) Sergej Razvodovskij/Shutterstock, SuriyaPhoto/Shutterstock, (middle left) Photosani/Shutterstock, (middle right) Booka/Shutterstock; **11:** Jeff Thrower/Shutterstock; **12:** (background) Alphaspirit/Shutterstock, (clockwise from top left) rubberball/Getty Images, Somos Photography/Veer, Payless Images/Shutterstock, Joshua Hodge Photography/iStockphoto; **14:** Fabrice Malzieu; **15:** Fabrice Malzieu; **16:** (top right) Martin Carlsson/iStockphoto, (top right photo shoot) charity myers/iStockphoto, (bottom right) 4x6/iStockphoto; **17:** (left) Ablestock.com/Thinkstock, (right) iStockphoto/Thinkstock; **19:** Jupiter Images/Thinkstock; **20:** (Lady Gaga) Helga Esteb/Shutterstock.com, (magazine cover) Maria Deseo/PhotoEdit, (monitor) Fotonium/Shutterstock, (paparazzi) Losevsky Pavel/Shutterstock, (middle) Jeff Schultes/Shutterstock, (middle background) echo3005/Shutterstock; **22:** (middle left) Karina Kononenko/Shutterstock, (top right) Howard Kingsnorth/Getty Images; **24:** (man and woman) Fabrice Malzieu, (café background) Shvaygert Ekaterina/Shutterstock; **25:** Fabrice Malzieu; **26:** (left wire) MalDix/Shutterstock, (right wire) donatas1205/Shutterstock, (background) ilolab/Shutterstock, (top right) Stockbyte/Thinkstock; **27:** (bottom left) jcjgphotography/Shutterstock; **29:** Jupiter Images/Thinkstock; **30:** (top right, people talking) Gina Sanders/Shutterstock, (top right) Viktor Gmyria/Shutterstock, (blog image) Shutterstock, (bookshelf) Ferenc Szelepcsenyi/Shutterstock, (middle left) Creatas Images/Thinkstock, (middle center) Gabe Palmer/Getty Images, (middle right) Huchen Lu/iStockphoto; **32:** (browser window) Shutterstock, (girl studying) Jack Hollingsworth/Thinkstock; **34:** Fabrice Malzieu; **35:** Fabrice Malzieu; **36:** (newspaper) Hemera/Thinkstock, (coffee beans) Gtranquillity/Shutterstock; **37:** (bottom) Tupungato/Shutterstock.com; **42:** (classifieds) Alex Slobodkin/iStockphoto, (businessman, top right) Dmitriy Shironosov/Shutterstock, (mother and daughter) Kzenon/Shutterstock, (middle left) Shutterstock; **44:** (top left to right) StockLite/Shutterstock, Collage Photography/Veer, c./Shutterstock, Jupiter Images/Getty Images, wavebreakmedia ltd./Shutterstock, (background) kakin/Shutterstock, (haircut) Jupiter Images/Thinkstock; **45:** Deklofenak/Shutterstock; **46:** Fabrice Malzieu; **47:** Fabrice Malzieu; **48:** (background) re_bekka/Shutterstock; **49:** (middle right) takayuki/Shutterstock, (bottom right) Sideways Design/Shutterstock; **51:** (bottom) mtkang/Shutterstock, (poster) Benoit Chartron/iStockphoto; **52:** (top, clockwise left to right) Aneal Vohra/Photolibrary, kak2s/Shutterstock, mangostock/Shutterstock, (fence) Johannes Kornelius/Shutterstock, (middle right) © Allison Shirreffs; **54:** (top background) James Thew/Shutterstock, (middle from left to right) Ocean Photography/Veer, (clockwise from bottom left) Phase4Photography/Shutterstock, michellegibson/iStockphoto, Tyler Olson/Shutterstock; **56:** (top left) Pakhnyushcha/Shutterstock, (top middle) Jupiterimages/Thinkstock, (top right) Distinctive Images/Shutterstock, (middle) Fabrice Malzieu; **57:** (middle) Fabrice Malzieu, (bottom right) © Steve Debenport/iStockphoto, (ribbon) Robyn Mackenzie/Shutte; **58:** (background) Tanor/Shutterstock, (top right) © Mercy Ships/Debra Bell, (bottom left) © Mercy Ships/John Rolland; **59:** © Mercy Ships/John Rolland; **60:** (top center) Blend Images/Shutterstock, (bottom left) Goodshoot/Thinkstock, (bottom middle) Karel Gallas/Shutterstock, (bottom right) Brand X Pictures/Thinkstock; **61:** (bottom right) Jupiter Images/Thinkstock; **62:** (girl in 3D glasses) Nejron Photo/Shutterstock, (money in phone) Slavoljub Pantelic/Shutterstock, (robot) Julien Tromeur/Shutterstock, (African American professor) Hemera Technologies/Thinkstock, (Amanda) Andresr/Shutterstock, (Oliver) iodrakon/Shutterstock, (Sam) Phil Date/Shutterstock, (Judith) holbox/Shutterstock; **63:** Valentyn Volkov/Shutterstock; **64:** IT Stock/Thinkstock; **65:** razihusin/Shutterstock; **66:** Fabrice Malzieu; **67:** Fabrice Malzieu; **68:** James Thew/Shutterstock; **71:** Kuzma/shutterstock

Text credits

Every effort has been made to trace the owners of copyrighted material in this book. We would be grateful to hear from anyone who recognizes his or her copyrighted material and who is unacknowledged. We will be pleased to make the necessary corrections in future editions of the book.

Corpus

Development of this publication has made use of the Cambridge English Corpus (CEC). The CEC is a computer database of contemporary spoken and written English, which currently stands at over one billion words. It includes British English, American English and other varieties of English. It also includes the Cambridge Learner Corpus, developed in collaboration with the University of Cambridge ESOL Examinations. Cambridge University Press has built up the CEC to provide evidence about language use that helps to produce better language teaching materials.